CAMBRIDGE

Brighter Thinking

Russia in the Age of Absolutism and Enlightenment, 1682–1796

A/AS Level History for AQA Student Book

John Oliphant

Series Editors: Michael Fordham and David Smith

CAMBRIDGE
UNIVERSITY PRESS

University Printing House, Cambridge CB2 8BS, United Kingdom

Cambridge University Press is part of the University of Cambridge.

It furthers the University's mission by disseminating knowledge in the pursuit of education, learning and research at the highest international levels of excellence.

www.cambridge.org
Information on this title: www.cambridge.org/9781316504352 (Paperback)
www.cambridge.org/9781316504369 (Cambridge Elevate-enhanced Edition)

First published 2016

A catalogue record for this publication is available from the British Library

ISBN 978-1-316-50435-2 Paperback
ISBN 978-1-316-50436-9 Cambridge Elevate-enhanced Edition

Additional resources for this publication at www.cambridge.org/education

Message from AQA

This textbook has been approved by AQA for use with our qualification. This means that we have checked that it broadly covers the specification and we are satisfied with the overall quality. Full details of our approval process can be found on our website.

We approve textbooks because we know how important it is for teachers and students to have the right resources to support their teaching and learning. However, the publisher is ultimately responsible for the editorial control and quality of this book.

Please note that when teaching the A/AS Level History (7041, 7042) course, you must refer to AQA's specification as your definitive source of information. While this book has been written to match the specification, it cannot provide complete coverage of every aspect of the course.

A wide range of other useful resources can be found on the relevant subject pages of our website: www.aqa.org.uk

Contents

About this Series

Cambridge A/AS Level History for AQA is an exciting new series designed to support students in their journey from GCSE to A Level and then on to possible further historical study. The books provide the knowledge, concepts and skills needed for the two-year AQA History A-Level course, but it is our intention as series editors that students recognise that their A-Level exams are just one step on to a potential lifelong relationship with the discipline of history. The book is thus littered with further readings, extracts from historians' works and links to wider questions and ideas that go beyond the scope of an A-Level course. With this series, we have sought to ensure not only that the students are well prepared for their examinations, but also that they gain access to a wider debate that characterises historical study.

The series is designed to provide clear and effective support for students as they make the adjustment from GCSE to A Level, and also for teachers, especially those who are not familiar with teaching a two-year linear course. The student books cover the AQA specifications for both AS and A Level. They are intended to appeal to the broadest range of students, and they offer not only challenge to stretch the top end but also additional support for those who need it. Every author in this series is an experienced historian or history teacher, and all have great skill both in conveying narratives to readers and asking the kinds of questions that pull those narratives apart.

In addition to quality prose, this series also makes extensive use of textual primary sources, maps, diagrams and images, and offers a wide range of activities to encourage students to address historical questions of cause, consequence, change and continuity. Throughout the books there are opportunities to critique the interpretations of other historians, and to use those interpretations in the construction of students' own accounts of the past. The series aims to ease the transition for those students who move on from A Level to undergraduate study, and the books are written in an engaging style that will encourage those who want to explore the subject further.

Icons used within this book include:

Key terms

Developing concepts

Speak like a historian

Voices from the past/Hidden voices

Practice essay questions

Taking it further

Chapter summary

About Cambridge Elevate

Cambridge Elevate is the platform which hosts a digital version of this Student Book. If you have access to this digital version you can annotate different parts of the book, send and receive messages to and from your teacher and insert weblinks, among other things.

We hope that you enjoy your AS or A Level History course, as well as this book, and wish you well for the journey ahead.

Michael Fordham and David L. Smith
Series editors

PART 1: PETER THE GREAT AND RUSSIA, 1682–1725

1 Establishing authority, 1682–1707

In this section we will look at the condition of Russia in 1682. We will consider the way in which it was governed, as well as the person of Tsar Peter himself. We will also look in some detail at the social and political structures, including the Church, the attempts at reform and the opposition to those attempts. In addition, we will take into account Peter's foreign policies and wars. We will look into:

- The political, economic and social position of Russia in 1682: the Tsars and the nobility; economic backwardness and serfdom; Russia as a traditional, Slav society.
- The Regency: the role of the Streltsy; Peter as joint ruler; the establishment of sole rule.
- Westernisation: influences on Peter as a child; the Great Embassy; the reasons for and significance of the development of St Petersburg.
- Early reforms: economic and financial; political and administrative; military; changes in society
- Opposition: the Church; the Streltsy.
- Foreign affairs and wars: wars against Turkey and Sweden.

The political, economic and social position of Russia in 1682

The Tsars and the nobility

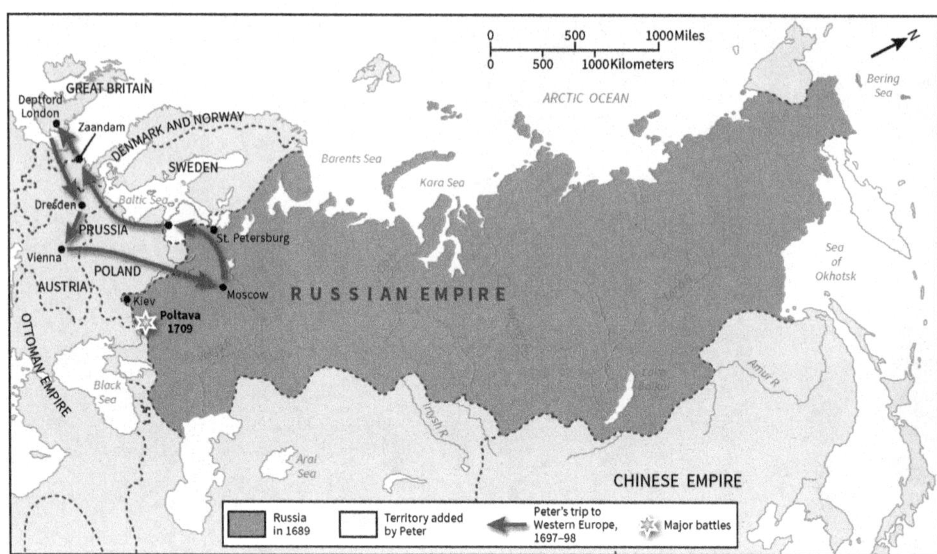

Figure 1.1: Russia at the end of the 18th century

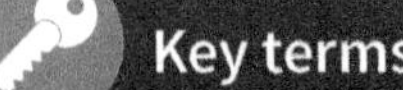

Key terms

Ottoman: the dynasty which governed the Turkish Empire. Often used as a name for the empire itself.

Khanate: a kingdom ruled by a khan, usually in southern or eastern Russia, usually Muslim, usually Mongol or Tartar foundations.

Autocracy: a system of government in which one person (the 'autocrat') has total power.

The state of Muscovy, the name still occasionally given to Russia in 1682, grew up in the centre of the great undulating plain which sweeps from eastern Europe to the Ural Mountains. It falls into three regions:

- North: tundra, a treeless region where the subsoil is frozen all the year round;
- Central: taiga, a coniferous forest;
- South: steppe, temperate grassland.

These regions stretch from Europe, across Asia to the shores of the North Pacific in three vast bands.

Moscow, the city upon which Muscovy was centred, lay on the Moscow River, a tributary of the southward-flowing River Volga, within the forested area. Muscovy was open to attack from all sides: from the Poles and Swedes to the north-west and west, from the **Ottoman** Turks (and their client **khanates**) to the south, and from Tartars, the descendants of the Mongol conquerors, to the east. Such a state must either expand or be overwhelmed. That in turn required a powerful military organisation and a strong, even ruthless, central government.

Russia thus emerged as an expanding **autocracy**. Tsar Ivan III ('the Great') (1462–1505) brought over two centuries of Tartar domination to an end, drove back the Polish-Lithuanian frontier westward, conquered the rival state of Novgorod to the north and even penetrated across the Urals into Siberia. His grandson, Ivan IV ('the Terrible') (1547–1584) reacted to a Crimean Tartar raid on Moscow by constructing a line of defensive forts from the River Dnieper to the Volga and by overrunning the khanates of Khazan and Astrakhan, thus linking the Volga to the

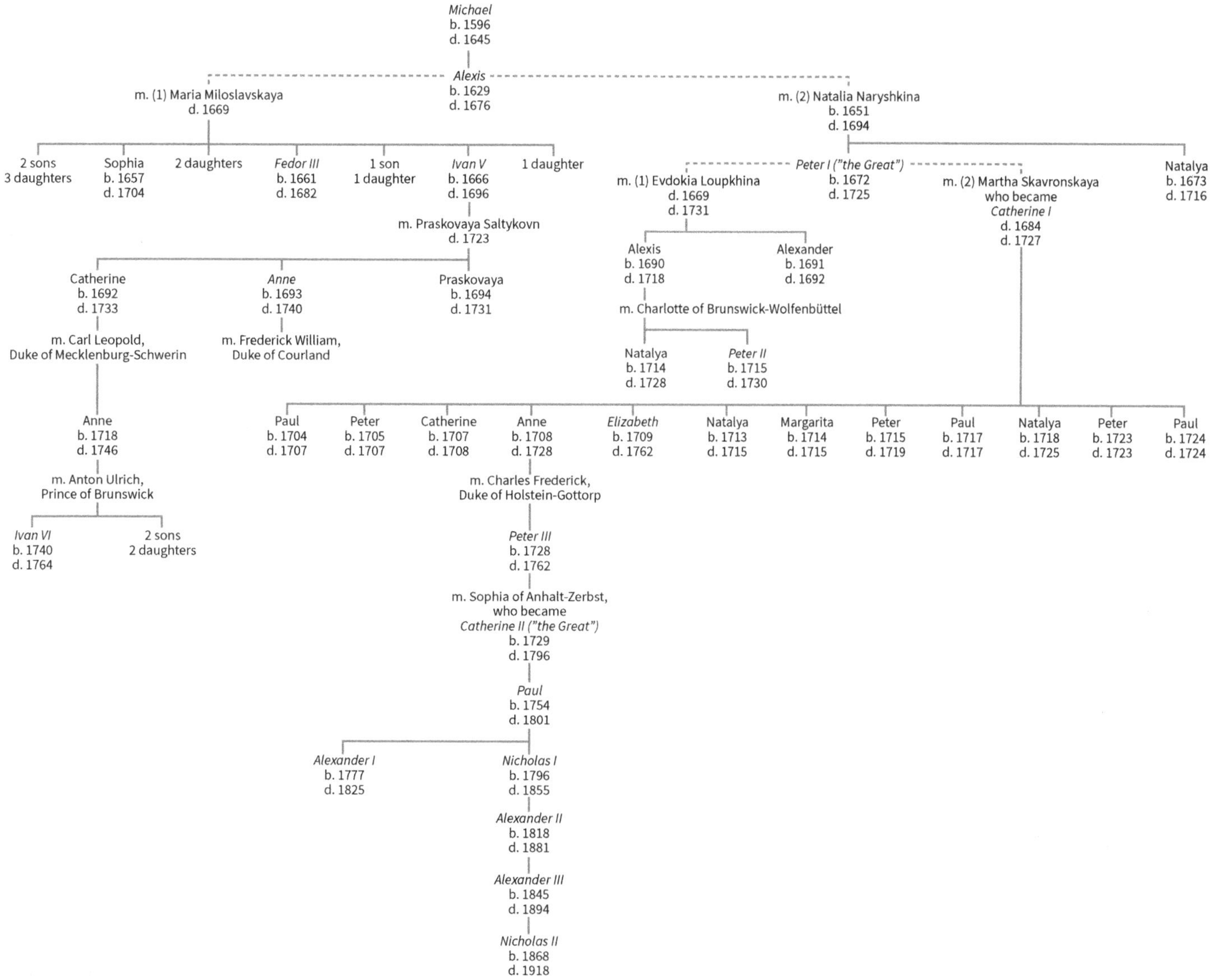

Michael
b. 1596
d. 1645

Alexis
b. 1629
d. 1676

m. (1) Maria Miloslavskaya
d. 1669

2 sons
3 daughters

Sophia
b. 1657
d. 1704

2 daughters

Fedor III
b. 1661
d. 1682

1 son
1 daughter

Ivan V
b. 1666
d. 1696

1 daughter

m. Praskovaya Saltykovn
d. 1723

Catherine
b. 1692
d. 1733

Anne
b. 1693
d. 1740

Praskovaya
b. 1694
d. 1731

m. Carl Leopold,
Duke of Mecklenburg-Schwerin

m. Frederick William,
Duke of Courland

Anne
b. 1718
d. 1746

m. Anton Ulrich,
Prince of Brunswick

Ivan VI
b. 1740
d. 1764

2 sons
2 daughters

m. (2) Natalia Naryshkina
b. 1651
d. 1694

Peter I ("the Great")
b. 1672
d. 1725

Natalya
b. 1673
d. 1716

m. (1) Evdokia Loupkhina
d. 1669
d. 1731

Alexis
b. 1690
d. 1718

Alexander
b. 1691
d. 1692

m. Charlotte of Brunswick-Wolfenbüttel

Natalya
b. 1714
d. 1728

Peter II
b. 1715
d. 1730

m. (2) Martha Skavronskaya
who became
Catherine I
d. 1684
d. 1727

Paul
b. 1704
d. 1707

Peter
b. 1705
d. 1707

Catherine
b. 1707
d. 1708

Anne
b. 1708
d. 1728

Elizabeth
b. 1709
d. 1762

Natalya
b. 1713
d. 1715

Margarita
b. 1714
d. 1715

Peter
b. 1715
d. 1719

Paul
b. 1717
d. 1717

Natalya
b. 1718
d. 1725

Peter
b. 1723
d. 1723

Paul
b. 1724
d. 1724

m. Charles Frederick,
Duke of Holstein-Gottorp

Peter III
b. 1728
d. 1762

m. Sophia of Anhalt-Zerbst,
who became
Catherine II ("the Great")
b. 1729
d. 1796

Paul
b. 1754
d. 1801

Alexander I
b. 1777
d. 1825

Nicholas I
b. 1796
d. 1855

Alexander II
b. 1818
d. 1881

Alexander III
b. 1845
d. 1894

Nicholas II
b. 1868
d. 1918

Figure 1.2: The Romanov family tree

Caspian Sea. However, on the steppe, Tartar cavalry was still superior to Russian forces, and in the west the state of Poland-Lithuania was too strong to disturb.

Thus the most dramatic expansion was eastwards beyond the Ural Mountains. Tsar Boris Godunov (1598–1605) and his successors' expeditions pushed eastwards through the forested vastness of Siberia against primitive tribes unable to match Russian arms. In 1639 a small band of **Cossacks** reached the Pacific, after which Russia pushed south. Southward Siberian expansion was only checked when Russians encountered the might of the Chinese Empire along the Amur River.

Key term

Cossacks: a member of one of the self-governing semi-military communities ('hosts') formed in southern Russia and Ukraine by refugees from Tsarist authority and serfdom. By the 18th century the Cossack hosts were loosely tied to the Russian state for military service.

The autocracy

Ivan III was the first ruler to call himself 'Tsar of all the Russias' and Ivan the Terrible was the first to adopt it as an official title. As an autocrat the Tsar had almost unrestricted power over his state and subjects, far beyond even that claimed by Louis XIV of France. Louis was an absolute monarch only within certain limits: he had to respect the privileges of the Church, the nobility and towns, privileges which generally carried exemptions from direct taxes. He could

Key terms

Zemsky zobor: 'Assembly of the Land', an elected body containing representatives of Church, nobility, towns and even some peasantry.

Boyars: the highest rank of the Russian nobility.

Duma: Russian council of nobles.

Patrimonial state: one in which the government has control over both public and private property, so that the two become almost indistinguishable.

'Modernisation': the theory of modernisation has been criticised as being applicable only to late 18th- and 19th-century Western Europe and North America. However, Professor Simon Dixon argues at the beginning of his book *The Modernisation of Russia, 1676–1825* that successive Russian rulers did indeed try to industrialise Russia and that the concept of 'modernisation' can be used to measure their progress.

Cottage industry: the production of goods such as yarn or cloth in rural homes rather than in factories.

ACTIVITY 1.1

Construct a diagram of the structure of Russian autocratic government. Use your own research to identify the names of the important *prikhazy*.

make laws without consulting a parliament but then had to submit them to constitutional courts for approval. Tsars knew no such restrictions: they could legislate, tax and conscript almost at will. The laws were executed by a civil service divided into ministries (*prikhazy*). The Russian parliament, the **zemsky zobor**, met rarely and not at all after 1684, while the Tsar's **Boyar** Council of nobles (or '**Duma**') was in decline and had no real power.

The Tsar could conscript the services and property of his subjects for state purposes, such as raising armies and building new cities, ports, fortresses and canals. The American historian Richard Pipes uses the term **patrimonial state** to describe the Russian autocracy, arguing that the Tsar had so much power over his subjects that state and private property were virtually the same. In a sense, the Tsar *owned* Russia and the Russians. Pipes's argument may appear rather extreme – he is a controversial figure – but it is certainly the case that in Russia private property was not protected and was frequently requisitioned.

Economic backwardness and serfdom

Muscovy began in the upper-Volga forests, producing honey, furs and beeswax, while conquests to the south yielded slaves and corn. The eastward expansion of the 17th century was driven by the fur trade. Ivan III opened the port of Archangel in the Arctic, thus enabling Muscovy to trade with Western Europe during the ice-free summer months. Exports of furs purchased Western metal-ware, including English cannon. The huge demand for furs encouraged over-hunting and thus the need for further eastward and northern conquest to reach fresh supplies. Ivan IV even managed to conquer the province of Ingria on the Gulf of Finland between 1558 and 1560, thereby opening access to the Baltic, through which about half of Russia's external trade passed. (Two decades later, Russia lost it again to Poland-Lithuania.)

Failure to make much headway against the Turks, Poles and Swedes highlighted the need for economic modernisation. Historians have often used the term **'modernisation'** to describe the process by which a state emerges from a largely agricultural economy, where industrial production is limited to **cottage industry** for local consumption, to one based on large-scale production in factories. With this process go urbanisation and the growth of an industrial middle class of businessmen and bankers, together with an industrial working class (or 'proletariat') to work in the factories and mines. The causes of this change are held to be a rising population, the availability of raw materials (such as iron ore and coal), abundant capital in the hands of a rising middle class, a free and mobile labour force, and good (usually waterborne) means of transport.

From the 1630s a number of iron works were established in the Moscow region and especially at Tula, a river port 120 miles (190 km) south of the capital, where Russia's major armaments works was founded in 1632. Linens came from the Tver and Moscow regions, Nizhny-Novgorod in the north produced leather, and salt came from Kama and the upper reaches of the River Volga. To get these enterprises off the ground technical expertise from abroad was needed, so foreign experts were encouraged to settle in Russia. By 1682 at least 20 000 of these immigrants were living in the country. But the result was modest: there were only about 21 factories, four of them owned by the state, in the whole of Russia. Even in 1700 Russia was still a net importer of iron. In 1682 the economy remained primitive and overwhelmingly agricultural.

Russia as a traditional, Slav society

The Orthodox Church

Orthodox Christianity parted company with Catholicism, the religion of the West, in the Middle Ages and Constantinople, the capital of the Greek-dominated Byzantine Empire, became its headquarters. By 1453, when Constantinople fell to the Turks, Orthodoxy was firmly established in Muscovy and subsequently the concept developed of Moscow being the 'third Rome' (following Rome itself and Constantinople), making it the new centre of true Christianity. Because of this concept, the close working relationship between Tsar and Church was seen as modelled on the approach adopted by Christian Roman and Byzantine emperors.

Russia could thus be described as a **confessional state** in that the autocracy drew much of its authority from the Russian Orthodox Church, while the state supported, and even directed, the Church. The head of the Church was the Patriarch of Moscow and All Russia, the Russian Orthodox equivalent of the Pope. He lived in Moscow and his clergy taught that the autocracy was ordained by God. While rulers tolerated the non-Orthodox and non-Christian peoples whom they conquered, other forms of Christianity were not encouraged and were sometimes treated harshly.

Tsar Alexis (1645–1676) and Nikon, the Moscow Patriarch from 1652, had instituted reforms to bring the Russian Orthodox confession into line with its Greek parent. Nikon brought in foreign scholars, corrected the texts used by the Church and introduced changes, such as sermons, into church services. The traditionalists, the 'Old Believers', who saw the changes as a Roman Catholic conspiracy to undermine Orthodoxy, rejected all of Nikon's reforms and broke away from the official Church. Old Believers were fiercely persecuted – by the late 1680s over 20 000 of them had been burnt at the stake – but they survived in significant numbers right through the Tsarist period (and, to the present day).

The eminent 19th-century Russian historian Vasily Kliuchevsky saw this 'Great Schism' as a nationalist revolt against Westernisation. For him it represented conservative refusal to accept that the Church, the spiritual voice of the third and last Roman empire, was in fact backward and isolated. Nicolai Riasanovsky, a late 20th-century Russian historian working in the United States, saw it as an attempt to rejuvenate the traditional faith, and as a protest against the growing and oppressive autocracy of the Tsars. All of these factors seem to have been at work but their relative importance is still a subject for debate.

The nobility

The boyars, the Russian aristocracy, were not an autonomous class but **service nobility**. Whereas in Western Europe there was a sense of mutual obligation between ruler and nobles, in Russia the obligations all lay upon the nobles, and upon lesser landowners and gentry. They held their estates and **serfs**, not by right, but in return for compulsory service to the state. Although some did acquire

ACTIVITY 1.2

How far was Russia changing by 1682? Prepare a presentation on this subject for discussion in class. You'll need to consider a range of factors, such as political, social and economic forces.

Key terms

Orthodox Christianity: the Eastern branch of Christianity which formally separated from the Roman Catholic Church in the 11th century after centuries of undeclared drifting apart

Confessional state: a country in which the government supports, and is supported by, an official religion and encourages or compels its citizens to follow that religion.

Service nobility: landowners who had to perform compulsory service to the state (in the civil service or as military officers).

Serf: an unfree peasant, bound to their lord's estate. They have limited freedom of movement but are not slaves. They are obliged to provide labour and other services to the landowner

Developing Concepts

Make a list of the characteristics of modernisation according to 'modernisation' theory. Use the contents of this chapter to decide how many of these characteristics applied to Russia in 1682. Use your answers to decide how far modernisation theory can be applied to the study of Russian history at this time.

Key terms

Petrine: an adjective describing things to do with a 'Peter'. In Russian history, this invariably means Peter the Great. 'Pre-Petrine' – before Peter the Great

Bondage: a socio-economic status in which the one bonded is fixed in their position by a system of inflexible rules and conventions which limit their freedom.

substantial wealth, most pre-**Petrine** boyars lived very simply in wooden houses with very basic furniture and comforts. Such men were generally poorly educated and their manners were often crude. As they kept moving around the country on state business, they had comparatively little chance or inclination to build up local power bases, or to improve their estates. In 1682 even the *mestnichestvo*, the complicated system of precedence which limited the Tsar's ability to appoint officials on merit, was abolished. This was not a class well placed to offer resistance to the autocracy.

Peasants and serfs

Serfdom was central to Russian economy and society. Serfs were unfree peasants, bound to their lord's estate; they were not slaves. They were obliged to provide:

- to the landlord: labour and other services;
- to the state: taxes, labour (when called upon) and military service (which could be rewarded with freedom).

These burdens could be very heavy and most peasants were very poor. Serfs, however, had distinct rights: they belonged to a self-governing village commune or *mir*, elected their own village elders, conducted law suits and (within limits) made contracts.

Slaves, who comprised about 10% of the population, had none of these privileges. They included:

- members of conquered populations;
- prisoners of war;
- destitute peasants who sold themselves into **bondage**.

Because slaves were not liable for taxes or conscription, they were of limited use to the state; and because the very poor, who might otherwise have sunk into slavery, were often supported in peasant households, slavery died out in the Petrine period. Peter himself converted his household slaves into serfs in 1723. Serfdom, on the other hand, became far more burdensome.

Serfdom became firmly established in Russia at much the same time that it died out in most of Western Europe. It came about because both landowners and the state wanted a settled population: Tsars wanted taxes and soldiers, landowners wanted labour. Between 1500 and 1700 about half the peasants became the serfs of private landowners and the rest became 'state peasants' – in effect, serfs of the Crown. It can be further argued that all peasants were serfs of the Crown in that the state had first call upon their taxes and labour. From this it has been suggested that landowners, being only temporary proprietors of their serfs, cared little for their welfare and exploited them mercilessly.

How much truth is there in this analysis? Lindsey Hughes, an eminent British historian of Russia, has her own view.

Speak like a historian

Lindsey Hughes is Professor of Russian History in the School of Slavonic and East European Studies in the University of London. She has written extensively on the Petrine period, including a biography of the Regent Sophia.

> Received wisdom (underpinned by most Soviet writing) teaches that the great mass of the ploughing peasantry were impoverished and downtrodden, a view apparently confirmed by many contemporary accounts . . . Leaving aside the true extent of [foreigners'] knowledge of Russian peasants, it is probably true that most peasants had few possessions and lived on a simple diet. But it should not be assumed that the institution of serfdom meant that peasants' lives were not valued. On the contrary, peasants had a high value to their owners (as chattels to be sold or as payers of rent and agricultural producers) and to the State (as taxpayers, army recruits and labourers). The problem is that the State and estate owners were often in conflict, with the interests of the former frequently taking precedence over the latter . . . How could all claimants to a peasant's output get their fair share while allowing the peasant to satisfy his and his family's basic needs? This dilemma became particularly acute under an active, expansionist, demanding regime like Peter's, in a country where there was a wealth of land, but of relatively low quality, and a dearth of manpower.[1]

Discussion points

1. What does Hughes appear to mean by the 'received wisdom' on the condition of the peasants?
2. Why and to what extent does she reject this 'conventional wisdom'?

Town-dwellers

The British historian M.S. Anderson, by defining a town as a settlement of only 1000 inhabitants, calculates that perhaps 5% of Russians were town-dwellers. Moscow, with 150 000–200 000 people, was quite large even in European terms, but apart from distant Astrakhan, no other town was more than a tenth that size. The death rate in these settlements was high: crowded conditions produced deadly plagues and wooden houses were vulnerable to devastating fires. Thus, although the urban population was steadily growing, it was proportionately much lower than in Western European countries.

Towns were not self-governing, partly because of their generally tiny size and partly because more than a third of them were military settlements created to protect the southern and eastern frontiers. Thus, Anderson argues, perhaps 50% of town-dwellers were military or civilian employees of the state. Towns did not have taxation privileges, there was no independent middle class – there were no more than 400 wealthy merchants in the whole country – and there were few cultural activities to encourage independent thought and action. Indeed townsmen were as legally bound to their towns, as serfs were to their estates: in both cases, bondage made taxation simpler.

Key terms

Bandit: an armed robber; banditry is the practice of armed robbery.

Streltsy: the outdated Russian military units, with special privileges, abolished by Peter I

Conservatism: an attitude that prefers to postpone and minimise any change, and is suspicious of innovation of every kind.

Exiles and renegades: the Cossacks

Cossacks were steppe-dwelling Russian pastoralists living beyond the bounds of the Russian state. Originally they had been either peasant refugees from the growing Russian serfdom, or communities displaced by the Tartars. Their name comes from a Tartar word meaning 'horseman'. In 1654, having rebelled against Polish rule, they placed themselves under Russian protection on condition that they always retained their autonomy. In time that autonomy was eroded and serfdom introduced. As a result, Cossack revolts were common. On the other hand, Cossack regiments were the backbone of the Russian cavalry and Peter I had close Cossack advisers.

The growth of serfdom encouraged large-scale flight to Cossack and other frontier communities, leading to the rise of banditry. **Bandits**, offering violent resistance to the ever-increasing demands of landlord and state, sometimes became popular heroes, sheltered by peasant communities. Given such widespread sympathy and the vast size of Russia they were almost impossible to eradicate.

Thus Russian society developed as a paradox. Alongside the immense and increasing power of the state there emerged a level of popular resistance among peasants, among the Old Believers and along the southern and eastern frontiers.

The Regency

The role of the Streltsy

In 1676, when Peter was four, his father, Tsar Alexis, died unexpectedly. On his deathbed Alexis confirmed his eldest living (but very sickly) 15-year-old son as Tsar Feodor III. Peter and his mother were sent to Preobrazhensky, three miles outside Moscow, and their chief political ally, Artamon Matveev, was exiled to the far north. Feodor's mother's family, the Miloslavskys, were in control. However, by 1682 they had been gradually edged out of power by politicians connected to Peter's mother's relations, the Naryshkins.

Developing concepts

For each of these important concepts, write down a definition and give an example of what it meant in the context of Russian society and government around 1682.

- Autocracy
- Service nobility
- Serfdom
- Confessional state
- Patrimonial state.

When Feodor died in 1682 the Naryshkins moved quickly to establish control. Feodor's brother Ivan was seven years older than Peter but, although not as helpless as has sometimes been suggested, he was an invalid incapable of ruling alone. It was not difficult to persuade a hastily assembled *zemsky zobor* to dutifully proclaim Peter as sole heir. However, the late Tsar Alexis had also left a daughter called Sophia, and she turned out to be a political force not so lightly brushed aside.

Sophia's main weapon was the **Streltsy**. This was a military force, some 55 000 strong in 1682, formed in the 16th century to introduce modern firepower into Muscovy's armed forces. Membership was hereditary. Members were allowed to live in their own homes instead of in barracks, they could take part in trade and they could produce alcoholic beverages for their own consumption. However, by 1682 they were becoming discontented and insecure. There were many Old Believers among them and they harboured deep distrust of foreigners and of the boyars. Such **conservatism** was combined with the Streltsy's suspicions that they were being superseded. Their critics regarded them as outdated and increasingly inefficient. They were therefore threatened (and felt threatened) by Peter's and his predecessors' experiments with more modern military methods. There were also genuine basic grievances. Some of their colonels often **embezzled** the men's pay, and the commander-in-chief, Prince Dolgoruky, was particularly unpopular. In 1682 it was not difficult for the Miloslavskys to encourage rumours that Feodor had been poisoned and that the Naryshkins meant to murder Ivan too.

Key terms

Embezzle: to covertly steal money entrusted to one's care, often by falsifying accounts.

Coup: a sudden armed seizure of power by a small group.

On 25 May 1682 thousands of Streltsy forced their way into the Kremlin. The ten-year-old Peter, his mother Natalia, Ivan and Matveev met them on the Red Staircase, where Natalia encouraged them to speak to and touch Ivan to prove that he was still alive. But her courage did not halt the **coup**. Matveev was hurled to the floor below and butchered with halberds; several Naryshkins and some boyars were hunted down, dragged to a place of public execution and hacked into small pieces. Across Moscow murder and looting raged unrestrained for over a week. Peter and Natalia were unharmed – Sophia clearly had no intention of doing away with them – and they retired once more to Preobrazhensky. On 25 May a new *zemsky zobor* duly proclaimed one brother as 'first' Tsar as Ivan V and the other as 'second' Tsar as Peter I, so that officially they ruled together.

ACTIVITY 1.3

Class debate: Which was the more important cause of the 1682 coup: Sophia's plotting or Streltsy grievances?

Peter as joint ruler

The joint rule of Ivan and Peter was, of course, a sham. Although government decrees were at first issued in their joint names, power really resided with Sophia, who was in practice Regent, or stand-in ruler, though she was never formally given that title. Her lover and chief adviser was Prince Vasily Golitsyn, a gentle cultivated man who lived in a strikingly Western style. Between them Sophia and Golitsyn brought in a number of far-sighted reforms. Legal procedure and the penal codes were made more humane and Golitsyn devised plans for educating young Russians abroad, for building a modern Western-style army and for easing the condition of the serfs. There was even a hint of a move towards gender equality: at some of his banquets women guests were entertained on the same terms as men. Though some of Golitsyn's aims were very close to those later espoused by Peter, his methods were quite different: Golitsyn preferred gentleness to relentless energy, humanity to brutal coercion.

In foreign policy, too, Golitsyn anticipated Peter's development of closer relations with Central and Eastern Europe. A treaty with Poland in 1686 confirmed the Russian acquisition of Kiev, and with it the conquest of the rich farmlands of northern Ukraine. Embassies were sent to no fewer than 11 European states between 1684 and 1688. In 1689, faced with the expulsion of the Russians from the Amur River basin, Golitsyn's government negotiated the Treaty of Nerchinsk with China. This was the first such agreement which implied equality of status, made by that empire with any foreign power, and the boundary it defined lasted for over 200 years.

The establishment of sole rule

Sophia always knew that Peter's existence was the greatest long-term threat to her rule. In 1684 she made Ivan marry, in the hope that he would produce an heir with a claim stronger than Peter's. She exchanged the unofficial title of 'Regent' for that of 'Autocrat', implying that her own status was as good as Ivan's or Peter's. In 1687

ACTIVITY 1.4

Evdokia Lopukhina was Peter's first wife. Use this book and your own research to compose a one-page biography for class presentation.

some of her adherents suggested another coup to put her on the throne, but she still stopped short of the obvious course: murder.

None of this, however, could keep Peter out of the picture for long. In 1688, when he was 16, he began to take an interest in government and attend meetings of the Boyar Council. It was now impossible to pretend that he was still a minor. In January 1689, aged 17, he married Evdokia Lopukhina, a bride chosen by his mother, whom he quickly made pregnant – so it appeared that the 'second' Tsar, not the first, was about to strengthen his position by producing an heir. Moreover, as we shall see, Peter possessed his own private army in the form of two regiments that he had developed at Preobrazhensky. At the same time, Sophia's position was seriously undermined by two failed campaigns, led by Golitsyn, against the Crimean khanate in 1687 and 1688.

In the late summer of 1689 Sophia, seeing that a showdown could no longer be postponed, planned another Streltsy coup. On the night of 7 August she set them in motion towards Preobrazhensky to seize Peter in his sleep and kill him. Warned at the last moment, Peter escaped to the monastery of Troitsa-Sergeev, 40 miles away and out of Sophia's reach. Troitsa-Sergeev became a base around which the Naryshkins and their allies rallied, while Sophia's forces dwindled. The fickle Streltsy were divided and hesitant: after all, Peter's conservative mother was now more to their taste than Sophia's reforming regime. In September General Patrick Gordon, a Scot in the Russian service and a friend of Peter's, together with some other foreign officers commanding new-style regiments, threw in his lot with Peter. Sophia's position was now hopeless. She handed over her advisers to Natalia's faction and retired to the hospitality of a convent just outside the Kremlin. Golitsyn was sent to the far north, where he died in 1714.

The roles of the joint Tsars were now superficially reversed. Ivan was ignored while Peter became the only Tsar who mattered. But, as Anderson puts it, he reigned but did not rule. Even during the coup against Sophia he had been the passive agent of his mother's faction. Now, and for five successive years, power was exercised by his mother, Natalia, and exercised in the interests of conservatism. Diplomatic contacts with the outside world, especially Poland, were wound down. The Jesuit priests previously admitted to serve the Catholics in the Foreign Quarter were immediately expelled. When Patriarch Joachim, who had wanted to expel all non-Orthodox foreigners, died in March 1690 he was replaced by the even more reactionary Adrian, Metropolitan of Kazan. Peter's failure to prevent this appointment was a measure of his impotence at this time.

However, Peter was powerless less because Natalia overruled him than because he was not yet much interested in governing. His central concerns were still primarily military and, increasingly, naval. He built small ships, partly with his own hands, on Lake Pleshcheev, some 200 miles from Moscow, where he spent as little time as possible. In 1692 he even had to be begged to return to receive an important embassy from Persia. He conscripted his Preobrazhensky soldiers to work as shipwrights and, for the first time, imported foreign experts to direct them. In 1693 and again in 1694 he visited Archangel, still Russia's only port, and saw the sea for the first time. Thereafter he lost interest in Lake Pleshkeev and fixed his mind upon an ocean-going navy under his Swiss drinking companion, Franz Lefort. With the exception of Gordon, his foreign companions were all like Lefort: adventurers of a crude ill-educated stamp with a strong penchant for heavy drinking and womanising. Central to this activity was his club of intimates, the 'Jolly Company', later titled 'The All-Joking, All-Drunken Synod of Fools and Jesters', to mock tradition in general and the Church in particular. Mentally and physically, the young Tsar was still at play.

Two deaths forced Peter to take a more active and responsible role. His mother's demise in January 1694 forced him to take some part in the wider concerns of government. When Ivan V died in 1696 he had no choice: he was now sole Tsar. However he was a Tsar of a type hitherto unknown. Rather than the traditional remote figure, hardly ever venturing beyond the Kremlin walls and surrounded by endless formal ceremony, Russians were confronted with a brash young man who despised tradition, yet had no clear ambitions of his own. The stage was set for a long vigorous period of unprecedented and often unwelcome change, too frequently backed by force.

Westernisation

Influences on Peter as a child

The most important formative event of young Peter's childhood was the terrifying coup of 1682. Forever after he loathed the Kremlin, and the memory made him shudder even in adulthood. He carried the mark – an uncontrollable

Voices from the past

Figure 1.3: General Patrick Gordon

General Patrick Gordon, 1635–1699

Born into a family of minor gentry in Aberdeenshire, Scotland, Patrick Gordon was typical of many poor Scots gentry who, unable to find military employment at home, sought service in the armies of other states. As a Roman Catholic he was doubly disadvantaged before 1660, when King Charles II was restored to the thrones of England and Scotland, and after 1688, when the Catholic James II was overthrown in the 'Glorious Revolution'.

Gordon received his university education at a Catholic Jesuit College in Prussia. From 1653 to 1660 he served in the armies of Sweden and Poland, changing sides three times, before finally entering the Russian service under Tsar Alexis. After a diplomatic mission to England, he distinguished himself in campaigns against the Turks and the Crimean khanate. In 1687–88, while stationed at Preobrazhensky, he befriended Peter and in 1689 his support ensured the success of Peter's coup. In 1694 he accompanied Peter on naval exercises out of Archangel and in 1697 was entrusted with the refortification of newly captured Azov. In 1698, during Peter's absence in the West, he crushed a dangerous Streltsy revolt. Peter thought very highly of Gordon and after Sophia's downfall paid him the unprecedented compliment of visiting him for dinner. For historians of Russia, the surviving volumes of Gordon's personal diaries are invaluable primary sources.

ACTIVITY 1.5

What were the long- and short-term reasons for Sophia's fall from power? Were any of these factors more important than the others?

Figure 1.4: Peter the Great as a child

facial twitch – for life. No wonder then that he dreaded and despised the Streltsy, and the primitive, ignorant and superstitious conservatism that they represented. With them he associated his half-sister, whom he hated and distrusted, and the entire Miloslavsky family. He spent the following years outside Moscow, not in an exile imposed by Sophia, but by choice.

Peter's main residence was at Preobrazhensky, a palace on the River Yauza, where he was isolated from court life and politics. Here he acquired no sense of the issues facing his future realm and certainly knew little if anything of Sophia's and Golitsyn's innovations. His Orthodox-based conventional education, which had already given him a biblical knowledge good enough to one day impress the Bishop of Salisbury, came to an end. Instead he developed in other directions.

Military games

When Peter had turned 11 in 1683, he had been given real guns for the first time and some small-scale cannon. In time he acquired a collection that took several carts to move it from residence to residence. He recruited servants and serfs into his own toy regiments, with which he could carry out mock parades, marches, battles and sieges. Out of these games grew two real regiments, the green-uniformed Preobrazhensky Guards and the blue-clad Semenovsky Guards, which in turn became the core of the reformed Petrine army.

The management of his regiments led Peter to acquire skills in military engineering and gunnery, knowledge that he could only acquire from foreigners in the Sloboda, Moscow's 'German' suburb, where foreigners were obliged to live. These were practical technicians, not scholars, who had learned their professions on the job, just as Peter was doing and continued to do throughout his life. Theodor Sommer schooled him in the handling of artillery and Franz Timmerman taught him navigation by the stars, arithmetic, ballistics and fortification. Timmerman was with him when he came across an old English boat, which the Dutchman Karsten Brand later repaired and equipped with a new mast and sails. Infinitely handier than the traditional Russian flat-bottomed river barges, the vessel gave birth to Peter's fascination with ships and the sea.

Thus by the age of 17 Peter had emerged as a vigorous master of multiple practical trades, with a smattering of foreign languages, a very inadequate formal education and a restless impatience with tradition.

The Great Embassy

In March 1697 Peter left Russia and did not return until September of the following year. Under the transparent pseudonym of 'Peter Mikhailov' he travelled via northern Germany to the Dutch Republic and to England, returning by way of Vienna, thus becoming the first Tsar to venture beyond the bounds of Russia. The journey raises two key questions:

1. Why did Peter undertake such a prolonged visit to the West? As we shall see in the following section, his early innovations had stirred violent resentment among Russian conservatives: there could not have been a more dangerous moment to have turned his back on his domestic enemies.
2. How far did Peter's experiences lead him to attempt to Westernise Russia?

Let's take those two questions in turn.

In part, the embassy was designed to secure diplomatic alliances with Western powers against the Turks. At bottom, however, Peter's main motive was probably to acquire the modern technologies he needed to transform Russia into a Great Power. In particular, as M.S. Anderson argues, he wanted to learn about shipbuilding, navigation, seamanship and indeed everything to do with the sea. Travelling incognito, and the very fact of leaving, were a demonstration of his contempt for formal precedence, tradition and status. Going as a member of the entourage, rather than as the formal head of the mission, might also have been an attempt to keep himself free to learn manual skills – in itself a deliberate challenge to Russian conservatism. In this Anderson is in agreement with much modern historiography. However, Lindsey Hughes suggests that it was partly an attempt to conceal his absence from Russia. Government decrees issued during the embassy were published in the Tsar's name, as if he were still in Moscow. Perhaps Peter's contempt for conservative views was not so reckless after all.

ACTIVITY 1.6

Construct a mind map showing the factors influencing Peter as a child and the inter-connections between them.

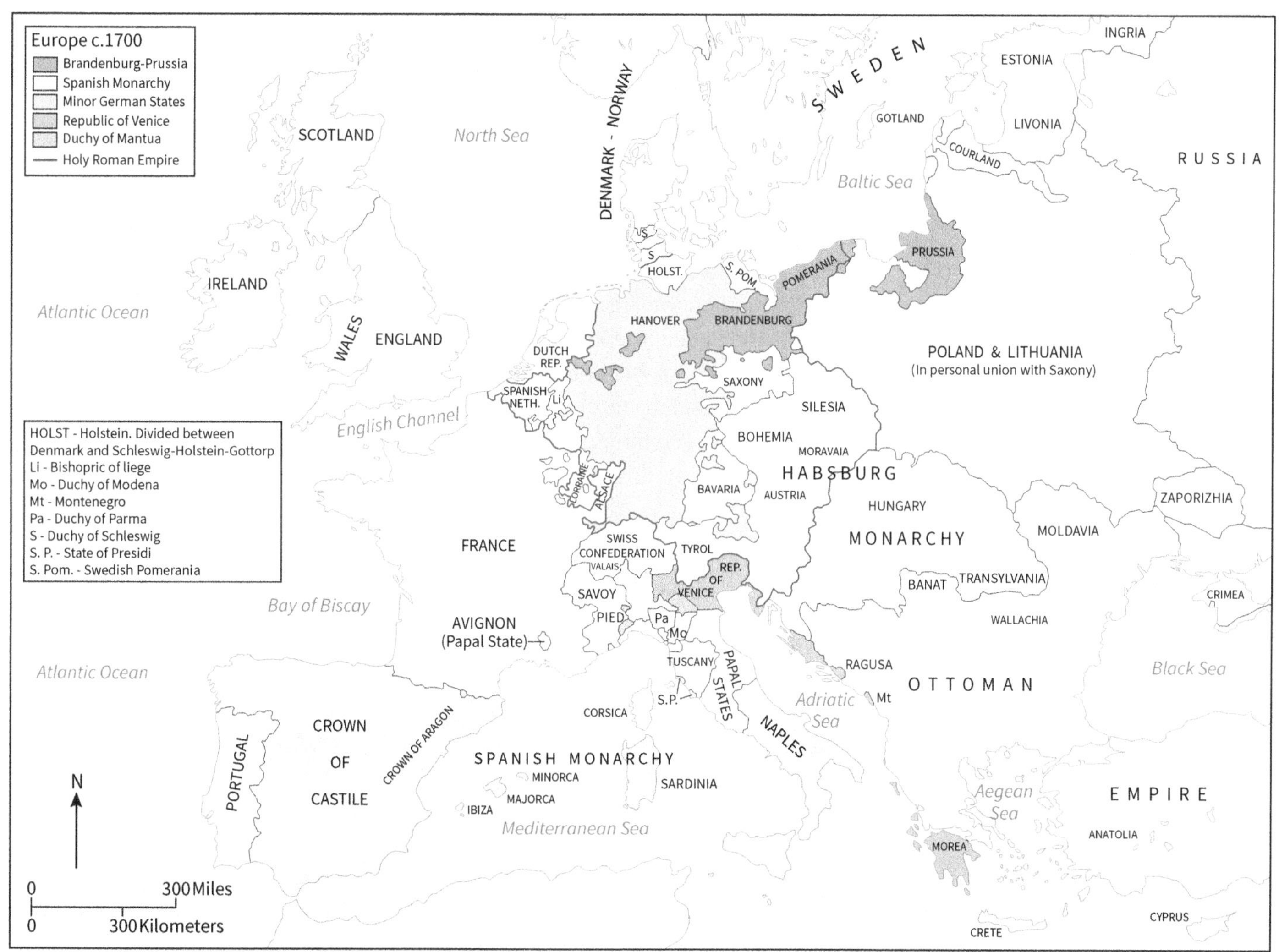

Figure 1.5: Europe at the end of the 17th century

Key terms

Expansionist: one who wishes his country to acquire more territory.

Habsburg Monarchy: the territories governed by the Archdukes of Austria, who were members of the Hapsburg family. Some of these territories, such as Austria and Bohemia, were within the Holy Roman Empire; others, such as Hungary, were not.

Elector: a member of the small group of German nobility with the traditional power to elect the Holy Roman Emperor.

Stadtholder: the head of state in the Dutch Republic.

Chancellor: a leading minister responsible to the ruler.

From Moscow it looked as though some kind of Christian alliance was not only possible but could be decisive. The Nine Years War, in which England, the Dutch and Austria had striven to check the **expansionist** aims of Louis XIV of France, was clearly about to end. Already, through his ambassador to Vienna, Peter had negotiated a three-year anti-Ottoman treaty with the Habsburg emperor and the Dutch. If a wider alliance could be constructed, Russia might well be able to expel the Turks from Kerch and gain access to the Black Sea, thus permanently strengthening Russia in the south. Moreover, Peter was worried about what might happen in Poland if, after the death of King John Sobieski, the French managed to put their own candidate on the throne.

None of this came to anything because neither England nor the Dutch Republic saw any reason to involve themselves in a new and distant conflict just to strengthen Russia. The West, including the **Habsburg Monarchy**, was preoccupied with the approaching death of the childless Charles II of Spain and the succession struggle that would follow. Peter came to see this all too clearly as his embassy progressed. An early treaty of friendship with Prussia was very far from an alliance, whatever the **Elector** Frederick William might have hinted in private. At Utrecht, William III, Dutch **stadtholder** and King of England and Scotland, was friendly and even gave Peter his favourite yacht, but would make no diplomatic commitments. In Vienna, talks with the Austrian **chancellor** failed to yield a commitment to honour the treaty of 1697.

Far more productive was the personal hands-on experience of Western technologies. In July 1697 Peter spent three weeks studying gunnery in East Prussia. In the Dutch Republic he became skilled in paper-making, etching and engraving, and met eminent Dutch scientists. He also worked for more than five months in an Amsterdam dockyard, learning how to build ships with his own hands. At Deptford, in England, he continued his shipbuilding studies, visited the Tower of London, inspected the Arsenal at Woolwich and was a guest of the elite scientific guild, the Royal Society. He probably understood very little of the abstract science he encountered, and paid little real attention to Western culture, political ideas and forms of government. As Anderson has it, 'it would be an error to suppose that this famous journey fundamentally changed Peter's ideas or even greatly widened his intellectual horizons'.[2] But he certainly did grasp that Western states' technologies and wealth were intimately connected with their military and, above all, naval power.

The impact of the journey on Peter

What impact did his experience have on Peter personally, and what were the impressions made by him on his hosts? At Riga, on the first stage of his pilgrimage, Peter asked to inspect and sketch the Swedish fortifications. His request was understandably refused and his way was barred by an armed guard. The Tsar, unused to being baulked, took umbrage and harboured a personal grudge which may have had some impact on his later decision to go to war with Charles XII. Elsewhere his intelligence, relentless questions and ready repartee won him admirers as disparate as William III of England and Scotland, the Bishop of Salisbury and the Electress Sophia of Hanover. He seemed to have an unquenchable thirst for everything from physics, to theology, to political science. On the other hand, the very same people were repelled by his own and his entourage's hard-drinking boorishness. The English diarist John Evelyn, whose house at Greenwich was hired for some of the Russians, found his lawn dug up, flower beds trampled, furniture burnt as firewood and family portraits used for target practice. On the whole Peter came across as a larger-than-life, immensely energetic, endlessly inquisitive barbarian from the very fringes of civilisation.

From Vienna Peter would have carried on to Venice, his third notional ally against the Turks, and possibly also to France. However, late in July 1698 he received a letter from the Governor of Moscow informing him that the Streltsy had risen yet again. Wrongly believing that his suspicions of his half-sister had been justified, he left abruptly for Moscow, determined to crush such violent, backward-looking and dangerous conservatism once and for all.

Peter had no use for English or Dutch social structures and certainly none for limited monarchy or republicanism. A trip to Oxford and occasional visits to theatres gave him only superficial impressions of wider Western culture. However, the experience powerfully confirmed him in his view that in order to make Russia a Great Power he must have people skilled in mathematics, navigation and other technical subjects. In 1701 he founded the Moscow School of Mathematics and Navigation, where foreign staff would train teachers for new **'cipher' schools** specialising in numeracy and geometry. Meanwhile, however, he needed foreign technical knowledge, foreign technicians and above all a Baltic port, a window on the West. That thinking lay behind the building of St Petersburg from 1703.

The reasons for, and significance of, the development of St Petersburg

St Petersburg ought to have been a catastrophic failure. The site – a labyrinth of waterways among the islands at the mouth of the River Neva – was unhealthy, subject to frequent flooding, surrounded by infertile soils and vulnerable to enemy attack. The Neva was free of ice for little more 30 weeks a year. Why then, did Peter follow his 1703 re-conquest of Ingria with the foundation of a city in so inhospitable a place? And why did the settlement, far from collapsing, thrive?

- The area was not such a bleak deserted place as subsequent legend has made out. There were a number of sizeable settlements there, including some great houses belonging to servants of the Swedish crown.
- The Neva was navigable and provided Peter's long sought-after outlet to the Baltic.
- The new port was to be the main point of entry for the modern technologies Peter needed to defeat Sweden decisively – and the West's window into Russia.
- St Petersburg was to be the embodiment of the very authority Peter was forging.

For all these reasons the city had to be magnificent. The first buildings were earthwork defences and some wooden huts, including one for Peter himself, but already he was planning magnificent buildings and attractive gardens. In a letter of June 1704 he acknowledged the arrival of four peony bushes, still in bloom, and ordered the dispatch of camphor, mint and other plants with strong perfumes. In Peter's mind St Petersburg was to be a 'Paradise'. There may have been an element of irony here when he used the word. Menshikov, the Governor of Ingria, knew all too well how cold, mosquito-ridden and dismal the place could be. Nevertheless,

ACTIVITY 1.7

Class presentation: what were Peter's motives for undertaking his Great Embassy?

ACTIVITY 1.8

Assess Peter's aims and achievements in making the Great Embassy of 1697–98.

Key term

Cipher schools: schools specialising in mathematics. established under Peter I.

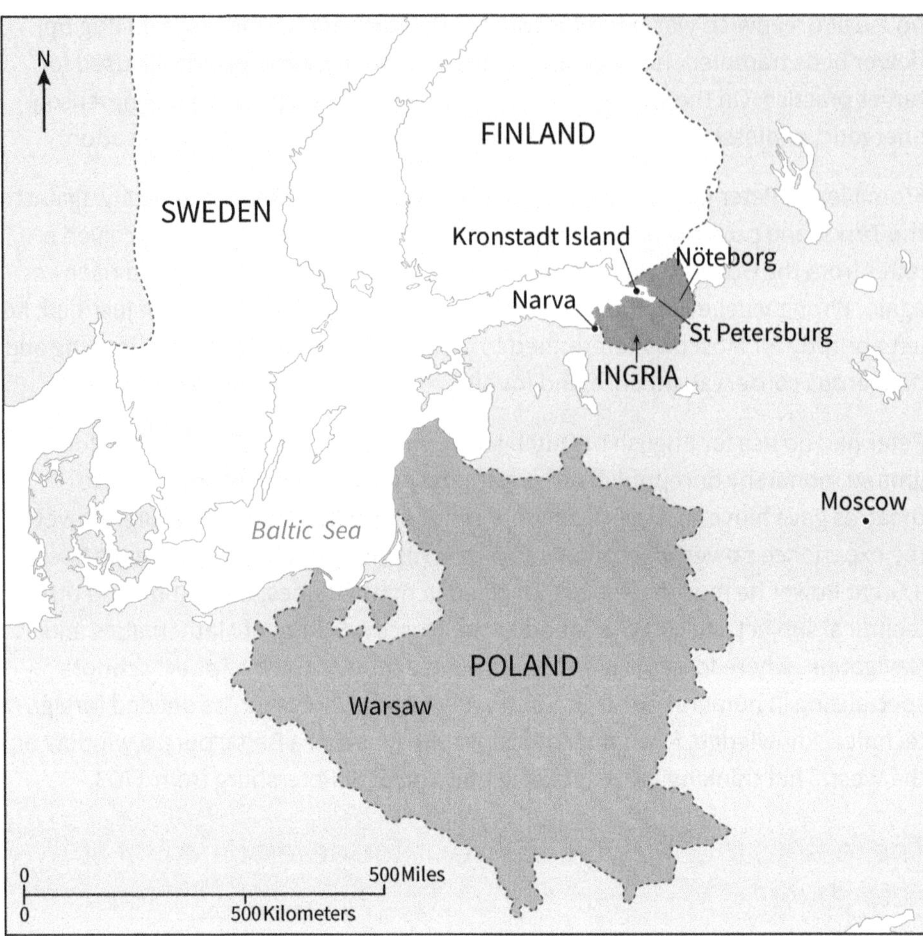

Figure 1.6: St Petersburg was in a defensible position on the Gulf of Finland, with easy access to the Baltic and the West, but was for some time vulnerable to Swedish attacks through Finland.

Key terms

Patriarch: the priest at the head of the Russian Orthodox Church

Third Rome: a term used for Moscow, or Muscovy. After the fall of Rome and then (in 1453) of Constantinople, and the end of the empires based on those cities, many Orthodox considered Moscow to be the last bastion of true Christianity

it is clear that Peter not only wanted to promote it as a showplace but, as Lindsey Hughes argues, saw its location as sacred Russian soil.

St Petersburg was also part of the Tsar's challenge to the established order in Orthodoxy. Moscow was the home of the **Patriarch**, the legendary **'Third Rome'**. Peter, wishing not to weaken the Church, but to bend it even more decisively to the state, assembled a band of mainly Ukrainian clergy who found ways to elevate the new city's spiritual status. Much was made of a legendary visit by St Andrew, himself a fisherman, to northern Russia. Then there were ship symbols: the ship of salvation on the sea of life, and St Peter's ship, the Church. Moscow might have been the Third Rome but St Petersburg was identified as the New Jerusalem mentioned in the Book of Revelation. The city was vital to Peter's counter-offensive against conservative accusations that he was the Antichrist.

For those who had to do the work, however, the new capital was no earthly paradise. From 1706 tens of thousands of conscripted workers were escorted to St Petersburg under armed guard and set to work rebuilding the fortifications in stone. The number recruited always fell short of those prescribed in Peter's orders – for 30 000 in 1706, 40 000 in subsequent years – and more died from overwork, exposure, disease and hunger. As James Cracraft points out, annual casualties may not have been as grim as foreigners' accounts and later legend claimed, but they certainly ran into thousands. The shortfalls had to be made up by drafting in even more hands from the furthest fringes of the empire: even gangs of Tartars from the far south could be seen toiling on the works. As in much else, Peter's determination was reflected in the ruthless driving of his people.

ACTIVITY 1.9

Use the evidence in this section, and your own personal research, to write an essay explaining why St Petersburg was so important to Peter in this period.

Early reforms

Economic and financial reform

Financial management

War was the main activity of government and it had to be financed through taxes. This was nothing new. Peter's predecessors had also had no other source of finance than ever-greater taxation. There was no sophisticated system of credit and nothing like the contemporary English financial revolution that had enabled William III and Queen Anne to confront richer and more populous France. The government expenditure figures for 1704 illustrate Peter's priorities.

Area of expense	% of total government expenditure
Military and naval	40.9
Civil service	37.6
Royal household	4.4
Diplomacy	2.1
Church	0.8
Educational, medical and postal services	0.5
All other items	13.7

Table 1.1: Government expenditure, 1704.

An efficient centralised system of collection, towards which previous Tsars had been feeling their way, was therefore a key priority in the effort to increase revenue. In 1699, between the Turkish and Northern wars, Peter introduced the *Ratusha*, a new office for the collection of revenues from the towns. The *Ratusha* replaced officials of 13 *prikhazy* and Peter (unsuccessfully) tried to get the merchant class to pay more for the limited autonomy that the change gave them.

Was Peter a 'mercantilist'?

Mercantilism is one of those terms coined by historians to describe particular historical phenomena, in this case certain economic ideas common in late 17th- and 18th-century Europe.

Broadly speaking, 'mercantilism' was a policy of favouring the protection of home industries through heavy tariffs upon foreign goods and heavy subsidies for home production. The aim was to achieve self-sufficiency both to increase the country's wealth and to improve its ability to fight and win wars. Peter's policies were certainly protectionist and driven by his military needs, but were they 'mercantilist'? Unlike Western states, Russia did not place much reliance upon foreign trade, let alone a favourable balance of trade, which would force foreigners to pay for the difference in precious metals or other forms of wealth.

In addressing the question of Peter's possible mercantilism, we have to acknowledge that, because the supposedly 'mercantilist' systems varied so much from state to state, some historians have wondered whether it is a useful term at all. The question will be addressed in greater depth in the next chapter.

'Forced industrialisation'

What was beginning to happen in Russia was a process of **forced industrialisation**, in which the state organised and directed industrialisation without significant help from private enterprise. In the first section of this chapter we saw that process already under way by 1682, and Peter's early efforts to support the war effort intensified it. Coal and iron-ore mines and iron-smelting works were established in the Ural Mountains, while around Moscow textile production for military clothing became important. However, as we shall see below, before 1707 such expansion hardly amounted to an industrial revolution.

Key terms

Forced industrialisation: industrialisation through state planning, compulsion and conscription.

Bureaucracy: a civil service, the officials employed by a government to carry out its orders.

Political and administrative reform

Boyar Council and *zemsky zobor*

The Russian machinery of government did not change fundamentally in this period, but the authority of the Tsar over it was certainly extended. The traditional Boyar Council was already in decay and clearly incapable of taking major decisions. Under Peter its membership shrank from 182 in 1689, to 85 in 1702. Of these, no more than 30 to 40 actually attended meetings after 1690, and even they were given no important business to transact. By 1704 the Council was effectively (though not officially) abolished. In its place Peter employed informal and ever-changing groups of advisers whose only power base was royal favour. Ministers could not use their parliamentary standing as a lever because there was no parliament: the last *zemsky zobor* met in 1684 to ratify the peace with Poland. Not only was a constitutional monarchy a near-impossibility under Russian conditions, but Peter was deliberately emasculating such institutions as did exist.

Civil service

Nor could the **bureaucracy** provide an effective brake on the Tsar. A *prikhaz* could cover either a specific area of policy (such as foreign affairs), or many aspects of government in a specific geographical area (such as Siberia). This produced conflicts of jurisdiction and, because individual departments could be created or abolished almost at will, there was no institutional culture capable of resistance. Foreign office officials, for example, had no strong traditions of mutual loyalty and tradition to be found in similar bodies in the West. It was even impossible to say, at any one moment, how many *prikhazy* there were; one estimate for 1699 gives a total of 44. It followed that a strong-minded Tsar like Peter could mould the civil service to his will with a minimum of fuss. He did so partly by appointing the same man to head up to six *prikhazy* at once. However, only a thorough overhaul of the whole system could produce the efficient government at which Peter aimed and for most of his reign he had no coherent plan for change.

At a local level, moreover, the grip of central government, though powerful and crushing when it worked, could be distant and sporadic. Provincial governors (*voevody*) often lacked local knowledge, were effectively beyond the day-to-day authority of Moscow and administered vast regions with sparse populations and poor communications. Here Peter's growing **absolutism** failed to function.

Key term

Absolutism: a system of government in which the ruler or ruling body has full powers to govern within certain limits,

Military reform

The disaster at Narva, where Peter's army was routed by a much smaller Swedish force and almost all of Russia's field artillery was lost, pushed the Tsar into a fury of military reforms. His measures were not, however, revolutionary. The Streltsy had been created in the 16th century to supplement the ill-trained cavalry levies; and the Streltsy in turn had been overtaken, from the mid-17th century, by new regiments, led mostly by Germans and modelled upon modern German practice. Those regiments 'of the new formation' in turn inspired Peter's own modernising efforts.[3] As M.S. Anderson has it, 'in military affairs, as in so many other areas, he accelerated and intensified a process of change which had begun long before he was born'.[4]

ACTIVITY 1.10

To what extent did Peter extend his authority over the mechanisms of government in the years 1682 to 1707? Draw a mind map reflecting both change and continuity.

Recruitment

Peter's first step in preparation for the Swedish war was taken in 1699, with the recruitment of volunteers and peasant conscripts to create new regiments. Every landowner who served in the armed forces had to provide one infantryman for ever 50 peasant households on his estates; civil servants had to produce one for every 30 households and for monasteries it was one in 25. This produced about 27 infantry regiments and 2 of **dragoons** (mounted infantry).

Key term

Dragoons: originally foot soldiers who rode to the battlefield but dismounted to fight. By the 18th century they were essentially cavalry able to fight on foot as well as on horseback.

The disaster at Narva showed that Russian discipline and leadership were still no match for the finest army in Europe and Peter redoubled his efforts. He set about raising 52 new infantry regiments. To replace the lost guns, about one-third of all the church bells in Russia were melted down and recast as cannon: 301 pieces were ready as early as November 1701. Nine new cavalry regiments were created by 1702. In 1704 Peter ordered the recruitment of former Streltsy into the new formations.

That more or less met the post-Narva emergency, but to win the long grinding war against the Swedes Peter needed a regular system of recruitment. Because most of the Russian population were serfs, voluntary enlistment could never bring in more than a tiny proportion of the numbers needed. Serfs might, with their master's consent, volunteer in exchange for their freedom, but the rigours of military service made this an unattractive option. Conscription therefore continued to be indispensable. In 1705 Peter twice demanded one young recruit from every 30 peasant households; in addition, on the second occasion, every 80 households had to provide a cavalryman. Evasion was common, usually by running away just before or just after recruitment, and Peter instituted detailed counter-measures. In 1705 it was decreed that one of every three deserters should be hanged and the other two flogged and sent to hard labour.

It was harder to find competent officers. Using foreigners was only part of the answer, as officers prepared to serve in Russia were generally those unable to find employment nearer home. In order to increase the number of native Russian officers, the following measures were taken:

- From 1698 the Preobrazhensky regiment ran its own officer school.
- From 1700 the larger landowners had to provide conscripts for officer training. Some of these young Russian cadets were sent abroad to learn their trade in Western armies. Most were trained in the Guards regiments.
- From 1701 gunners were taught in a specialist artillery school.
- From 1702 Peter insisted on recruiting only skilled foreign officers.
- In 1709 the first academy for engineers was set up in Moscow.
- Following 1711 and the Pruth campaign, many senior foreigners were sacked.
- From 1721 only Russians could obtain commissions in the artillery.

Thus, although their overall quality was never outstanding, Russia became self-sufficient in officers.

Arms and equipment

Arming such numbers without an adequate industrial and technological base meant that, initially, weapons – flintlock muskets and bayonets, and modern artillery – had to be obtained abroad. The loss of over 150 guns at Narva stimulated a huge production effort, so that by 1709 Russia could produce over 15 000 muskets and a good proportion of its own artillery, and had reached near-self-sufficiency in gunpowder, grenades and bullets. However, some weapons still had to be imported and most of the artillery was tied up in garrisons or in siege batteries: Peter's armies tended to fight from strongly fortified positions to avoid facing the Swedes in open battle. Consequently there were never more than 150 field guns. Moreover, older edged weapons such as pikes continued to be important. Peter's armies were still nowhere near his desired level of modernisation and self-sufficiency in firearms.

Western uniforms were introduced in an ad hoc, haphazard way, as circumstances and available resources dictated. In 1696 the Preobrazhensky Guards were prescribed a set of clothes to be paid for by the men's former masters, but they were the only unit officially so equipped. Later the Preobrezhensky wore green tunics and the Semenovsky blue. Other regiments dressed their men in whatever colours – indeed, in whatever clothes – came to hand. Food supply, especially in the south, where victory tended to go to the army whose provisions lasted longer, continued to be a nightmare.

Training

Training such numbers of raw recruits was another problem never wholly solved in the early years. The Guards were highly effective – at Narva they were the only units to stand their ground – but the ordinary line regiments were not. Peter's 1708 'Instructions for Combat' laid enormous stress on accurate shooting because, as the British military historian J.F.C. Fuller long ago pointed out, Russian marksmanship was abysmal and discipline no better. Linear battle formations were complex and took a long time to master. Together, these factors meant that Russian forces in the open field were highly vulnerable. But within the context of a siege the Russian artillery quickly became highly proficient. In 1698 there were few skilled Russian gunners and many foreign experts were employed; in 1705 a British general in Peter's service reported that he had never seen any army use their siege pieces better than the Russians in 1704 at Narva. Yet the artillery was the exception that proved the rule. Lack of training, skill and discipline were more common.

ACTIVITY 1.11

Make a web diagram showing the changes Peter brought into the Russian army. How extensive were these changes?

The navy

Peter's pride and joy, the entirely new Russian navy, was far more revolutionary and its early development was as haphazard as the army's. In the beginning it was a personal fascination, with its roots, so Lindsey Hughes argues, in Peter's childhood with model ships and pictures. Later it became a kind of status symbol, a sign of Russia's emergence as a Great Power as well as a useful adjunct to the army's land operations.

The first Russian-built ship was laid down at Archangel in the early 1690s but the construction of a battle fleet did not begin until the first Russian campaign against the Ottoman port of Azov, at the mouth of the River Don, in 1695. The siege ended in failure because Ottoman ships were free to supply the fortress by sea. For the second campaign in 1696 Peter set about building powerful river- and sea-going flotillas. Orders were placed in foreign yards for two 36-gun frigates, four fireships and 130 longboats. At the Preobrazhensky wharf 22 **galleys** were built, on the pattern of a Danish model, for riverine and shallow inshore water work. They were carried in sections to Voronezh, where they were reassembled in a specially commissioned yard. At the same time Peter produced a disciplinary and signal manual, the 'Order of Naval Service', the first of many minutely detailed documents setting out each rank's duties. The new fleet had a resounding success when it prevented a Turkish seaborne relief effort; thereafter, Peter's siege works and artillery, both directed by Austrian experts, quickly forced Azov to surrender.

Key term

Galleys: light vessels equipped with fore-and-aft sails and oars, enabling them to manoeuvre in light or unfavourable winds or in calms.

With the onset of the Swedish war Peter had hundreds of small craft built in the estuaries of the northern rivers and on Lake Ladoga (1701), and in 1703 production of sea-going warships began at a yard at Olonets. When St Petersburg was founded, the island of Kronstadt was developed as its protective naval base and a shipbuilding wharf was established on the Neva.

All this was possible only with the aid of foreign expertise. From 1697 noblemen were sent abroad to study shipbuilding, seamanship and navigation, but such were the manpower demands elsewhere that only tiny select groups could be spared. Peter's embassy abroad in 1697–98 gave him practical experience in all these branches and led to the establishment of the Moscow School of Mathematics and Navigation, which was staffed by British experts. Flag officers might be British, Norwegian or Greek.

Was the effect of the fleets proportionate to all this effort? The Azov fleet, which Hughes calls 'a white elephant', fought no major actions after 1696.[5] Shipbuilding there continued until at least 1700 but the quality of materials and workmanship was poor. The Baltic fleet assisted at the siege of Nöteborg in August 1701 but did little thereafter because the Swedish naval threat in the Gulf of Finland was minimal. Ships were constructed out of unsound oak or even pine, their timbers were fastened with inferior iron, and too often foreign officers were corrupt. Only after 1712 did the fleet become really useful and, even then, dependence upon foreign experts continued.

ACTIVITY 1.12

Was Peter's new navy fundamentally a toy? Using two columns, list the factors on both sides of the argument before reaching a conclusion.

Changes in society

We can now see that in these early years the most important social change was the accelerated expansion and deepening of serfdom and its associated burdens. Even though Patriarch Nikon's reforms of the Church were sustained by the state, Old Believer piety and tradition were still strong. Penetration of Russia by foreign ways and faiths was strictly controlled, and changes encouraged by the court – Western dress, shaving, drinking tea and coffee – were few in number and shallow. In any case, as long as Russia was struggling to hold its own against Sweden, any changes were hurried and unsystematic. Arguably, continuities were still stronger than the forces of change.

Opposition

We have seen that, even as the grip of the government over its people tightened and widened, so various kinds of existing opposition grew or developed. Among these were:

- peasant banditry within the control zone;
- unrest among the Streltsy;
- the activities of Cossacks and other bands of exiles on the fringes.

These strands of resistance were interlinked and were often fed by Old Believer sympathies. Here we will look in greater depth at the Old Believers and the Streltsy. How did such opposition arise and how effective was it in the years up to 1707?

Key term

Old Believers: Christians who rejected Patriarch Nikon's reforms of the Russian Orthodox Church

The Church

Opposition within the Church came from **Old Believers**, who felt that Peter, by encouraging liturgical change, as well as consorting with and aping foreigners, was drawing Russia away from Orthodoxy and towards Rome. As early as 1690 Patriarch Joachim and the unknown author of a pamphlet entitled *Against the Latins and the Lutherans* made this point. A little later Patriarch Adrian denounced shaving and tobacco, and in 1696–97 Father Araamy of St Andrew's monastery advised the young Tsar to consult churchmen rather than laymen, to stop his childish games and to beware of the largely foreign 'intriguers and embezzlers' around him. There were many more short anonymous letters which expressed much the same fears and phobias, including the suspicion that the real Tsar had been imprisoned and replaced by a German substitute. The new calendar introduced in December 1699 only reinforced such forebodings and by 1700 Peter was accused of being the Antichrist, the Devil himself. It was said that citizens should resist by refusing to pay taxes or do state service, and should revolt with the aid of the Streltsy.

Savage punishments such as flogging, the cutting out of tongues and the quartering of a bishop failed to silence such stories. In many cases, as Boris Uspensky has argued, misunderstandings came about because different values were attached to some words. For example, Peter, by taking the title 'father of the fatherland', a secular title derived from the Roman Empire, seemed to be claiming priestly powers.

ACTIVITY 1.13

Presentation for class discussion:

'What caused the Streltsy revolt of 1698? Which factors were most important?'

The Streltsy

The bloody Streltsy assault on the Kremlin in May 1682 and the attempted removal of Peter in 1689 were far from the end of Streltsy turbulence. They disliked all of Peter's innovations:

- desire for a navy;
- Western clothes;
- friendships with foreigners, especially with Franz Lefort.

As M.S. Anderson puts it, they were deeply alarmed by 'his wholesale and brutal rejection of the behaviour proper to an orthodox tsar'.[6] In February 1697, shortly before Peter started on his **Great Embassy** to the West, his spies discovered that a Streltsy colonel called Ivan Zickler, two leading boyars and a Cossack leader were plotting to murder Peter and put a boyar on the throne. The plot came to nothing and Zickler and his friends were brutally executed, but the resentment lingered. Indeed, the ruler's withdrawal from Russia, apparently for his own amusement, only deepened conservative anger. In the spring of 1698, while Peter was away, regiments destined for Azov and other remote postings sent representatives to Moscow to protest. The rejection of their petition sparked another futile revolt in June. The mutineers intended to destroy the foreign suburb of Moscow and break up the new regiments designed to supplant them, and probably to put Sophia on the throne.

Key term

Great Embassy: Peter I's journey to the West, 1697–98.

Anderson rightly describes this insurrection as a 'disorganized and leaderless explosion of helpless resentment', easily put down by loyal forces.[7] However, the news of it made Peter break off his tour in order to hurry back to Moscow and deal with this permanent source of danger once and for all. He also suspected that Sophia had been behind the revolt. Thus the significance of the 1698 rising lies not in the event itself, but in the thorough and brutal reprisals taken afterwards. Even before he arrived in Moscow in August, investigations ordered by Peter were under way. Dissatisfied with the progress and conduct of this investigation the Tsar ordered fresh trials to begin in September, not to establish guilt or innocence but to extract information about the Streltsy's motives and confederates.

The process went on until February 1699. Hundreds of Streltsy were tortured, usually by being flogged until their backs were raw and then being slowly roasted over a fire. Fourteen specially constructed torture chambers processed about 20 men a day, after which they were executed. The executions, too, were grim: many of the victims were broken on the wheel. Severed heads were displayed on poles and three men were hanged (and left hanging for months) outside Sophia's Novodevichy convent window. Altogether 1182 men were executed and 601 banished. Peter, however, did not rely upon making dramatic examples: the Moscow Streltsy regiments were broken up and their former members distributed to remote garrisons.

Sophia, though she never confessed to involvement in the revolt, was a particular target. As long as she remained a prisoner and a credible alternative to Peter, she would continue to be a focus for conservative plots and revolts. She was put on trial, Peter himself taking part in her interrogation, if not in her torture, and forced with one of her sisters to become a nun.

Anderson argues that such vigorous measures produced their own new wave of resentment and, as Lindsey Hughes points out, the dispersal of the Moscow Streltsy may have been counter-productive.

One of the remote places where resentments festered was Astrakhan, where exiled Streltsy mingled with rough-and-ready fugitives and migrants who had come to work in fisheries and the salt works. Old Believer sentiment and continual rumours that the real Tsar had been replaced by a German imposter inflamed this explosive mix. The immediate cause of revolt was Peter's enforcement of the decrees on beards and dress. Streltsy and other Old Believers who appeared in traditional dress found themselves barred from churches. When they saw head-shaped wooden blocks used for shaping wigs – another foreign fashion – they mistook them for pagan idols.

On 30 July 1705, Streltsy overwhelmed the garrison's guards and massacred their officers and local officials. Their aim was to march on Moscow, kill the Tsar's wicked 'German' advisers and their families, find the Tsar and make their key demands. These included the restoration of the Old Believer version of Orthodox Christianity and the withdrawal of the shaving and dress decrees. Refusal would reveal the Tsar as a fake who could be legitimately killed. Like the rebels of 1696 and 1698, however, they were not at all anti-Tsarist.

This was a far more serious matter than the chaotic rising of 1698. Despite failing to rouse the Don Cossacks, the rebels captured two significant towns and attracted some local support. Peter was sufficiently alarmed to make concessions, including a pardon. When the rebels failed to respond he used military force to crush them and took high-profile retribution. More than 42 men were beheaded locally and another 45 died under interrogation; 272 died in Moscow, 30 of them on Red Square. Even then the dispersed Streltsy were a threat. Anderson points out that their influence was at least partly behind the Don Cossack revolt that began in 1707 and which will be dealt with in the next chapter.

Key term

Holy League: an Austro-Polish-Venetian alliance formed in 1684 against the Ottoman Empire.

Foreign affairs and wars

Wars against Turkey

The Holy League

In 1686 Sophia's Foreign Office, directed by Vasily Golitsyn, made a permanent treaty of peace with Poland. Poland gave up her claims to Kiev, Smolensk and other disputed territories in Ukraine. In return, Russia paid Poland 146 000 roubles and agreed to go to war against the Turks and the Crimea. In this way Russia joined the **Holy League**, an Austro-Polish-Venetian alliance (approved by the Pope) formed in 1684 against the Ottoman Empire.

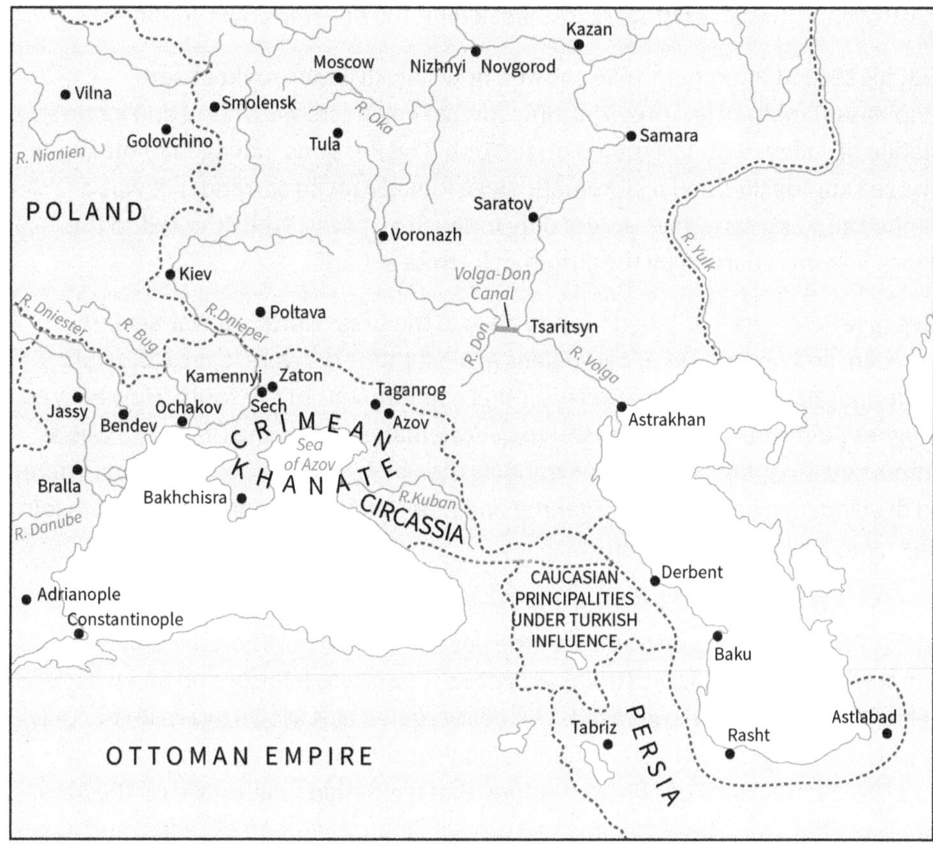

Figure 1.7: Russia and the Ottoman Empire

The campaigns of 1687 and 1689

In 1687 and again in 1689 Golitsyn led invasions into the Crimea. On both occasions Russia's allies provided disappointingly little assistance. Worse, Russian supply systems proved inadequate to support huge forces over such a distance and the armies had to withdraw. The second retreat was a disaster: vast numbers of horses and men were lost to thirst and disease. As we have seen, although Sophia ordered that Golitsyn be welcomed as a hero on his return to Moscow, his failure sparked the coup that removed Golitsyn and Sophia, and made Peter sole ruler in Russia.

Peter now suspected that his allies were planning to make a peace without him and he steered clear of military operations for almost six years. But then, in 1695, he launched a major offensive not against the Crimea but against the Turkish fortress of Azov at the mouth of the River Don. Lindsey Hughes suggests three reasons for this renewed conflict:

- to increase Russia's (and Peter's) prestige abroad;
- to strengthen his bargaining power with his allies;
- to check Turkish raids into Ukraine.

Peter's first campaign in 1695 achieved none of these goals. The Russians failed to cut off Azov from the sea; the Turks were able to resupply and reinforce it almost at will. The Russian command was divided and there was an alarming degree of technical incompetence. A mine intended to demolish the Turkish defences destroyed a Russian earthwork instead, killing 130 of Peter's own soldiers.

But his second attempt in 1696 showed how quickly Peter could absorb unpleasant military lessons. This time foreign engineers were hired and a massive flotilla of galleys was assembled on the Don. The Russians managed to **blockade** the sea approaches and a systematic siege forced Azov to surrender. It was a limited success: Azov gave access only to the Sea of Azov, while the exit to the Black Sea was guarded by the Ottoman fortress at Kerch.

Key term

Blockade: military and/or naval action to prevent access to or from a fortress or port.

Because Peter later switched his priorities to the Great Northern War against Sweden, and because later campaigns against the Turks were less successful, historians have underestimated his initial commitment to the south. However, as Hughes points out, there is reason to believe that, to Peter, the Black Sea was as important an outlet to the wider world as the Baltic. He spent considerable energy in developing a new base at Taganrog and made elaborate plans for canals to join the rivers Volga, Oka and Don.

In 1697 the Turks offered Austria a separate peace, at the very moment when Vienna was becoming distracted by the negotiations to partition the Spanish Empire in the West. The Austrians accepted, Russia was left isolated and what was left of the Holy League collapsed. The peace signed at Karlowitz gave Russia only a truce, although the other partners gained considerable territories. It was only in 1700, by the Treaty of Constantinople, that the Sultan finally gave up the Azov region to the Tsar. The Ottomans had proved far tougher than expected and it was over a decade before Peter resumed his southern ambitions. Meanwhile he turned north against the Swedes, seeking a Baltic outlet to the wider world, perhaps not as his primary objective, as is often assumed, but as an alternative.

Wars against Sweden

The beginning of the Great Northern War

In 1699 Peter set about constructing a Baltic alliance against Sweden:

- Augustus, King of Poland and Elector of Saxony, was anxious to reverse the long decline of Poland, due to the growing power of the Swedes.
- Frederick of Denmark-Norway was in competition with Sweden for domination of the western Baltic.

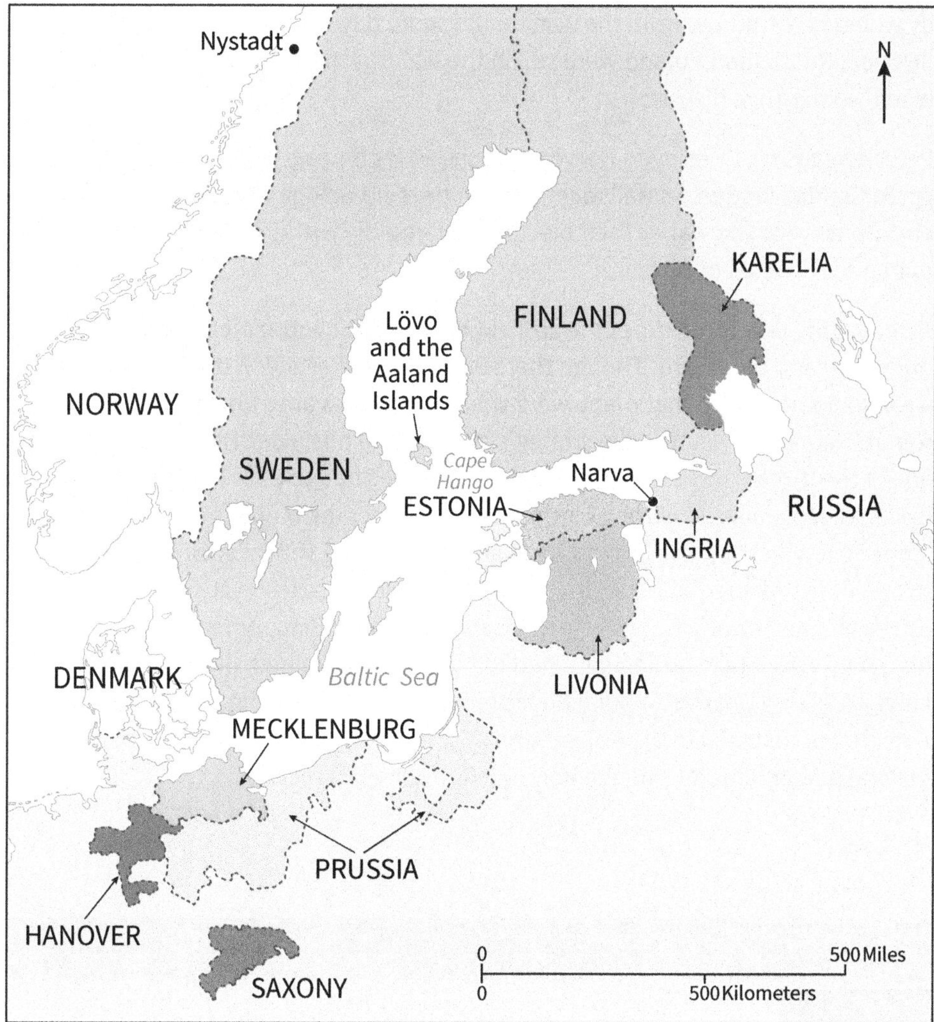

Figure 1.8: States involved in Great Northern War

Together they hoped to partition the Swedish Empire. Russia might then regain Ingria and with it a Baltic port, more convenient and ice-free for longer than Archangel.

There were five major weaknesses to this plan:

1. The allies did not concentrate their forces and failed to cooperate closely.
2. Peter's army was, despite his reforms, not yet sufficiently well armed, trained or disciplined to face a modern Western force. In contrast, the Swedish army was regarded as the best in the world.
3. Peter was inexperienced and made strategic and tactical errors.
4. The English and Dutch provided Charles with naval support, vital when it came to moving troops around the Baltic.
5. Peter was confronted with a young enemy possessed of extraordinary determination, strength of will and military talent.

First Charles turned on the Danes. An Anglo-Dutch naval squadron covered the landing of 10 000 Swedish troops at Copenhagen, just when most of the Danish army was in Holstein to the south. King Frederick IV signed the Treaty of Travendal, by which he withdrew from the war, on the same day that Russia declared war on Sweden. Russia and Poland were still in the war but their failure to cooperate fully would soon prove disastrous.

Peter's forces now besieged Narva while the Poles beleaguered Riga. But when Charles landed a small relief army in the Gulf of Riga the Poles, never as enthusiastic for the war as their elected king, rapidly withdrew, freeing Charles to march to the relief of Narva.

Peter's army was three times the size of Charles's, but was far less disciplined, organised and equipped. Though there was plenty of artillery, the gun carriages were so poorly made that many were shaken to pieces after firing only a few rounds. Moreover Peter made strategic and tactical mistakes. He failed to defend any of the three passes through which the Swedes had to pass to reach Narva, preferring to construct strong earthworks to protect the rear of his army while he carried on with the siege. But the wall and ditch facing the Swedes were too long to be defended adequately at every point, allowing Charles to choose his point of attack. Finally, aware that the Swedish army numbered no more than one-third of his own, Peter fatally underestimated the tough, determined and talented Swedish king. Expecting Charles to build up his forces cautiously before risking an attack, Peter left to investigate the Poles' behaviour at Riga, leaving an experienced general officer, Charles Eugène Baron de Croÿ, in command.

Voices from the past

Figure 1.9: Augustus II

Augustus, King of Poland and Elector of Saxony

Born in Dresden, the Saxon capital, in May 1670, Augustus became Elector of Saxony in 1694. In 1698, having made the necessary conversion from Protestantism to Catholicism, he was elected King of Poland-Lithuania, with Russian support. In 1700 he joined Peter I and the Danes in their war against Sweden, only to find himself attacked by Charles XII of Sweden and forced to abdicate in 1706. He was re-elected, again with Russian support, in 1709. He died in 1733.

His first election was supported and financed by Russia and Austria. Though an unreliable ally, his long struggle against the Swedish invasion saved Russia from early invasion and gave Peter time to reform the Russian armed forces. After his restoration, Poland became more or less permanently dependent upon Russia.

Figure 1.10: Alexander von Kotzebue, *The Battle of Narva, 1700*. This dramatic picture, showing the Russians fleeing from the Swedish onslaught, was painted almost two centuries after the event it depicts. Nevertheless, it gives an idea of the confusion, as well as of the arms and equipment of early 18th-century armies.

Some historians have seen this as an act of cowardice, or at least of the panic of a young and inexperienced ruler. There may have been an element of this in Peter's mind but it is more plausible to argue, as does Richard Pipes, that it was the sensible action of a leader who had to consider not just his own forces, but those of his allies as well. Moreover, Peter's career is littered with instances of outstanding physical courage.

For two days the armies were immobilised by a blizzard. Then, on the third day, the wind changed and the snow was blasted into the faces of the Russian defenders. Charles saw his chance and struck at once. Two Swedish columns broke through the overstretched Russian lines; Peter's centre and left dissolved into panic. The Swedes then destroyed the Russian army. In all between 8000 and 10 000 Russians were killed and many more were captured, along with all of Peter's artillery.

ACTIVITY 1.14

Produce a mind map showing the connections between the long, short and immediate causes of the Russian defeat at Narva.

Now list these causes and arrange them in a **hierarchy** of importance.

Figure 1.11: This French engraving shows the Russian defences and the two Swedish attacking columns. Note that the Russians had their backs to the river, making a safe retreat almost impossible.

Key term

Hierarchy: a social or political system composed of grades or ranks arranged one above another.

The Polish campaigns

Charles could now have secured a separate peace, knocking Russia right out of the war before turning to deal with the Poles. Peter certainly tried to find a mediator but, Hughes argues, Louis XIV wanted to keep the northern war going in case the Swedes joined his British, Dutch and Austrian adversaries. France pitched her terms – Cossack help for Hungarian rebels against Austrian rule and a massive loan to France – far too high. The English and Dutch feared that Charles would support the French if peace came, while the Austrians were glad to see Russia busily occupied. Thus Anglo-Dutch efforts to reach an agreement with Sweden were half-hearted and unsuccessful.

M.S. Anderson, however, contends that both sides wanted to hire Swedish and Saxon troops and therefore *did* want peace in the north. They were also alarmed by the war's continuing disruption of the trade in naval stores – pine trunks for masts, pitch for waterproofing and flax to make canvas for sails – essential for keeping their ships at sea. He points out that William III of England and Scotland offered mediation as early as 1700 and that his offer was accepted by Peter in May 1701. The stumbling blocks were Charles's determination to deny Russia any Baltic coastline whatsoever and Peter's resolution to keep a Baltic port whatever the cost.

Charles wanted the war to continue. He was contemptuous of Russian military capability – reasonably, in view of the Narva fiasco – and wanted to break the power of Augustus of Saxony and Poland. Therefore he turned south with the aim of installing a pro-Swedish Polish king and creating a buffer zone between Russia and the Swedish Empire. However, Augustus's armies proved much tougher than Charles had expected and from 1701 Russia supported him with 15 000–20 000 troops, money and supplies of gunpowder. It was not until 1704 that Augustus was deposed in Poland and the Swedish candidate, Stanisław I Leszczyński, elected; and it was 1706 before Saxony, the real base of Augustus's power, was conquered and Augustus finally surrendered.

Thus Peter not only survived but managed to score a series of minor successes in 1701–02, clearing a way to the Baltic and founding St Petersburg at the mouth of the River Neva in 1703. He also carried out a series of energetic military reforms, so that when Charles set out to invade Russia in 1707 Peter was ready for him.

ACTIVITY 1.15

In separate columns, list the differences between the positions of Hughes and Anderson respecting different countries' attitudes towards ending the Great Northern War. Offer an account of these differences.

Further reading

M.S. Anderson's *Peter the Great* (2nd edition, London: Routledge 2000) is a very well written and readable short account of the reign by a veteran historian of 18th-century Europe. From there you might do research into specific areas by dipping into Lindsey Hughes's long, detailed and perceptive *Russia in the Age of Peter the Great* (New Haven and London: Yale University Press, 1998). Richard Pipes's *Russia Under the Old Regime* (London: Penguin, 1995) is difficult and opinionated but does throw up some interesting ideas. A much shorter and more easily digested survey of the whole reign is S.J. Lee's *Peter the Great* (London: Routledge, 1993) in the Lancaster Pamphlets series.

Timeline

1682	Ivan V and Peter I established as co-Tsars. Beginning of the regency under Sophia
1689	Fall of Sophia
1696	Death of Ivan V. Azov captured from the Turks
1697–98	Peter's 'Great Embassy' to the West
1698	A revolt by the Streltsy brutally crushed
1700	Outbreak of war with Sweden. Russians defeated at Narva
1703	Foundation of St Petersburg
1704–05	Revolt in Astrakhan
1707	Charles XII of Sweden begins his invasion of Russia.

Practice essay questions

1. 'Very little changed in Russia in the years 1682 to 1707.' How valid is this statement?
2. How far would you agree that Peter's early domestic reforms were entirely the products of warfare?
3. To what extent was opposition to Peter in the years 1682 to 1707 driven by ideology?
4. 'Between 1682 and 1707, Russia became more deeply divided between traditionalists and modernisers.' How far do you agree?
5. 'Peter was able to assert his authority in Russia solely through the support of foreign mercenaries.' Explain whether you agree or disagree with this statement?
6. In the years 1682 to 1707, how far was Russian expansionism aimed at the Turks rather than against the Swedes?
7. With reference to the extracts below, and your understanding of the historical context, which of the two extracts provides the more convincing interpretation of the originality and effectiveness of Peter's early military reforms?

Extract A

Russia's strength lay under the surface and the initial underestimation of Peter's chances by allies and enemies alike was entirely understandable. Russia's army was in the process of modernisation, and previous experience demonstrated how difficult that was. The use of mercenaries in the Time of Troubles and the Smolensk War (1632–4) was a failure. Later on Tsar Alexis used European officers to train Russian soldiers, infantry and cavalry, in the new techniques of warfare, fighting in formation and using pikes to supplement musket fire. The change was not complete, however, and Peter had to start anew in the 1690s. Older elements remained, such as the Russian gentry cavalry, even operating in considerable numbers through the early years of the Northern War. The speed of change meant a lack of trained officers, whom Peter recruited abroad, but that system had its own difficulties. Unless modernisation was thorough and rapid, the changeover could create even greater confusion, as the first battle of Narva demonstrated.

Source: Paul Bushkovitch, 'Peter the Great and the Northern War', in Dominic Leven (ed.), *The Cambridge History of Russia: Volume II: Imperial Russia 1689–1917* (Cambridge: Cambridge University Press, 2006), 492–493.

Extract B

In fact from the 1630s onwards part of the Russian army was reorganised into 'new formation', or 'new model', regiments comprising infantry, lancer and dragoon units trained and commanded by foreign officers and organised upon foreign lines . . . It was these new-style units, rather than the [Streltsy] (a more or less hereditary corps of 'regular' troops who ran their own businesses during peacetime), who provided a model for future reform. Vasily Golitsyn's army in the Crimea in 1689 had thirty-five infantry and twenty-five cavalry regiments (lancers and dragoons) of this 'reformed' variety, with forty-five [Streltsy] regiments and Cossack auxiliaries. As the latter figures suggest, the numbers that Peter managed to recruit were not exceptional. In 1552 Ivan IV arrived to conquer Kazan with 150 000 troops and 150 pieces of artillery. With regard to 'professionalism', even before its abolition in 1682 the Code of Precedence was regularly suspended for individual campaigns, allowing promotions to the higher military ranks to be made on merit, and foreign officers trained and led the new-formation troops.

Source: adapted from Lindsey Hughes, *Russia in the Age of Peter the Great* (New Haven and London: Yale University Press, 1998), 64–65.

Taking it further

Up to 1707, how far was domestic reform in Russia driven by the needs of war and foreign policy?

Chapter summary

You should now understand the extent to which Russia was isolated from other countries in Europe, while also connected to them by trade and war. You should have begun to make informed judgements about the extent to which Peter I was able to establish himself securely on the Russian throne by 1707. You should be evaluating the extent to which Russia became a major power in the same period. You should have been comparing the interpretations of historians, and have begun making your own informed judgements about them. You should now have mastered:

- the political and social structures and forces at work by 1682
- why the Regency came into being, its achievement and failures and why it collapsed
- the extent to which Russia was 'Westernised' between 1682 and 1707
- how far Peter was able to extend his autocratic authority in this period
- the sources and effectiveness of different types of opposition
- the extent to which Peter was able to undertake successful military operations and expand Russia.

End notes

1 Hughes L. *Russia in the Age of Peter the Great.* New Haven and London: Yale University Press; 1998, 161–162.

2 Anderson MS. *Peter The Great.* London: Pearson Education; 1995, 44.

3 Anderson MS. *Peter The Great.* London: Pearson Education; 1995, 94, translating the contemporary Russian expression *novogo stroya*.

4 Anderson MS. *Peter The Great.* London: Pearson Education; 1995, 94.

5 Hughes L. *Russia in the Age of Peter the Great.* New Haven and London: Yale University Press; 1998, 86.

6 Anderson MS. *Peter The Great.* London: Pearson Education; 1995, 44.

7 Anderson MS. *Peter The Great.* London: Pearson Education; 1995, 45.

2 Increasing the glory of Russia, 1707–1725

In this section we will look at Peter the Great's reforms to the economy and political system in Russia. When doing so, it will be important to look at how things remained the same, as well as how things changed. We will consider the nature of the opposition to these changes. We will also look in some detail at the changing role of the Orthodox Church. We will again take into account Peter's foreign policies and wars, and consider the reasons and extent of Russia's emergence as a Great Power. In considering the successes and failures, we will need to ask to what degree the autocracy was strengthened between 1707 and 1725. We will look into:

- Economic and financial reforms and their success.
- Orthodoxy and developments in the Church: attempts to increase the power of the Tsar.
- Changes to central and local government; the reform of the army and the introduction of the Table of Ranks and the Service State.
- Social developments, Westernisation and extent of change by 1725.
- Opposition: Astrakhan; Bashkir; Don Cossacks; Tsarevich Alexis.
- Foreign affairs and wars: wars with Sweden and Turkey; involvement in European conflicts.

Economic and financial reforms and their success

A mercantilist state?

The term 'mercantilism' was invented at the end of the 18th century by a French economist and finance minister. Since then it has proved a slippery term with many definitions. However, historians are generally agreed that 'mercantilism' involved a partnership between the state and a vigorous, self-confident class of merchants and entrepreneurs. The state regulated trade to increase its military power, while businessmen received protection against foreign and even local competition. The state became stronger, while producers became wealthy. These aims were backed by a large quantity of theoretical writing, which stressed the importance of economic self-sufficiency and a favourable balance of foreign trade.

In the Cold War period (1945–1989) Soviet (Russian) historians strove to prove that Petrine economic reforms were distinctly Russian and owed nothing to Western mercantilist ideas. It may be no coincidence that, meanwhile, some Western historians tried to argue in the opposite direction. In 1962 Simone Blanc claimed that Peter's protectionist policies, aimed at economic self-sufficiency, were 'national in aim and mercantilist in method'.[1] For Alexander Gerschenkron, a Russian-born American working at Harvard University, Russia was part of a Europe-wide pattern of mercantilist economic development aimed at increasing the power of the state. Any differences, such as the very limited influence of Western economic theory or the spread of serfdom, were simply responses to local conditions. Russia was therefore a mercantilist state, if one with its own peculiar version of mercantilism.

There is some justification for the views of Blanc and Gerschenkron: some of Peter's efforts did indeed look like mercantilist measures:

- Bullion exports continued to be illegal.
- Foreign merchants operating in Russia had to buy their roubles with precious metals.
- Private enterprise was encouraged through subsidies and tariff protection.

However, other scholars have had their doubts. They argue that in Russia mercantilist theory counted for little:

- The state played an overwhelming role.
- The merchant class had to be bullied rather than encouraged.
- Massive compulsion was needed to provide an adequate workforce.

Even at the time, the British economic historian M.E. Falkus preferred to use the term 'forced industrialisation'.[2] M.S. Anderson denies that Peter 'can be considered a mercantilist in any real sense of that vague term', especially as he had little acquaintance with Western economic thought.[3] Lindsey Hughes has similar reservations, pointing out that Peter's vast library included only two treatises on economics, neither of which he properly understood.

ACTIVITY 2.1

As you work through this section, note down the key events for Russia's economic development between 1707 and 1725 and organise them into a timeline. Not all the relevant dates are listed at the end of the chapter.

Developing concepts

Use your own research and the material available in this book to assemble evidence for and against the proposition that Peter's policies were mercantilist.

Financial reforms: paying for the wars

Currency

As we have seen, Peter began the debasement of the Russian coinage as early as 1698. The silver content of coins fell rapidly. From 1704 to 1717, 20 roubles' worth of copper coins were struck from every 6–8 roubles' worth of copper. In 1723 the content was lowered even further.

Taxation

Peter's inventiveness when it came to indirect taxes did not abate. **Imposts** were placed on inns, bath-houses, beards (varied according to social rank), Russian dress, weddings, ferries and horse collars; and the state established monopolies over the supply of salt and tobacco. The most important innovation of all was the 'soul' or poll tax, a levy on every individual peasant, townsman and merchant, first mooted in 1718. Its primary purpose was to raise the extra 4 million roubles needed to support the army now that the war with Sweden was nearly over and troops were increasingly being quartered on Russian soil. To implement it a new time-consuming census was needed and consequently the tax was not levied until 1724. In the long run, however, by making taxation across and within the three broad social categories more equal, and so blurring and simplifying class distinctions, it had profound effects upon the social structure of Russia.

Key terms

Imposts: taxes, usually customs duties

Pood: a Russian measure of weight equivalent to about 36 lbs or 16.3 kg.

Tariff: a tax placed on imported goods.

The economy

Industry

The main driver of industrial growth continued to be the needs of the state. Iron and non-ferrous metallurgy continued to expand so that by 1716 Russia, a net importer of iron in 1710, had become a net exporter, and by 1725 was positioned to become the world's leading iron producer. By the end of the reign the Urals boasted around 76 iron foundries producing 800 000 **poods** of pig-iron a year.

Woollen textiles for clothing the armies continued to be important and, because so much cloth produced by cottage industry was too narrow, peasant weavers were ordered to use looms that turned out to be too wide for their dwellings. Subsidies were used widely, even to encourage the production of luxuries such as glass, velvets and silks for the royal court. From 1724 Russian industries were sheltered by high **tariffs** amounting to 50%–70% of the value of the goods.

Voices from the past

John Law, 1671–1729

Peter may even have considered creating a paper currency as a way around his bullion problem. In 1721 he invited John Law (a Scots banker who had settled in Paris in 1714 and the author of one of those economic treatises in the Tsar's library) to come to Russia. Law, an early believer in paper money, had risen to become Controller General of French royal finances and had established a powerful bank empowered to raise taxes and print bank notes. Unfortunately, the bank printed too much money and caused massive inflation – something the Controller General had not foreseen – and Law became a refugee. In the light of that background, Peter's invitation represented a bold initiative by a far-seeing ruler or, more likely, an impulsive gesture made in ignorance.

All of this required vast numbers of workers and those workers had to be conscripted. Conscription was not unknown in Western Europe, where soldiers and those on the fringes of society – criminals, vagrants, and unemployed and homeless beggars – could be mobilised for industrial projects or transported to work on colonial plantations. In Russia, however, the absence of a large pool of mobile, free labour meant that compulsion had to be used on a massive scale. A distinctly Russian method was to **ascribe** whole villages to the service of particular factories, almost always ones founded by the state itself. The natural resistance of landlords to ascription, which deprived them of their own workforces, meant that only four private factories were ever ascribed serfs. However, from 1721 individual industrial businesses, but not their owners, were permitted to purchase villages. Such serfs, known as 'possessional peasants', suffered conditions much worse than those experienced by ascribed state serfs or, by those who continued to till the land for their masters.

Key term

Ascription: Although serfs were largely tied to their village and owner, the government could use the power of ascription to allot them to a specific (government-chosen) task, even while, on paper, they remained a member of their original village.

Agriculture

Peter and his ministers paid far less attention to farming than to industry. It is true that some improving initiatives were taken. In the newly conquered Baltic territories Peter had encountered the scythe, which, with its long handle, enabled the reaper to work upright and was thus more efficient and less painful to use than the sickle to which peasants were accustomed. Thousands of scythes were imported for distribution. The area of cultivated land grew, partly because landlords were encouraged to relocate their peasants onto unoccupied (and more productive) land in southern and border areas. As a consequence, internal trade in grain grew significantly, as did the trades in flax and hemp. However, few of the gains were directly due to Peter's intervention and those initiatives that he did take were incoherent, short-lived and often frustrated by conservatism.

Other initiatives were:

- sheep and Silesian shepherds, experts in shearing and preparing wool, were brought into Kazan;
- horses were brought in from Persia and government stud farms set up;
- Italian experts in silk weaving were settled in Russia.

But a few thousand scythes, and small numbers of foreign experts and animals did not amount to a transformation. One reason for this limited effort was that government gave farming a far lower priority than industry. The other, possibly even more important, reason was the deeply ingrained conservatism of the peasants, who valued tradition above improvement and (understandably) suspected that the new techniques were part of a plan to exploit them even more thoroughly than before.

Figure 2.1: Pieter Bruegel the Elder, *The Harvesters*, 1565. Dutch reapers using scythes 150 years before Peter tried to introduce them to Russia

Foreign and internal trade

Peter's maritime enthusiasms, and the examples of the Dutch Republic and Great Britain, led him to see a merchant marine as a key to great prosperity. His efforts, however, were all failures. Russian merchants and ship-owners:

- could not beat the freight rates of their foreign rivals;
- could not insure their vessels and cargoes as cheaply;
- could not raise capital at such favourable rates;
- lacked their competitors' accurate knowledge of changing Western markets.

Trade with the West therefore tended to be passive: it was conducted with foreign merchants in Russian ports, not in London or Amsterdam. Peter's 1723 attempt to set up a Russian chartered trading company foundered, like an earlier one in 1699, on the obstacles listed above.

The few maritime commercial ventures that did bear fruit had immediate government support. One such was the dispatch of two frigates bearing Russian goods to Livorno, the great Italian trading port, in 1717. Another was the creation of a company to trade directly with Spain, a potential source of American bullion to a Russia critically short of precious metals. Three ships provided by the state were sent out to Spanish ports laden with Russian products. Neither initiative was followed up: it was mid-century before Russia could boast a viable trade with the Mediterranean.

However, elsewhere there were some successes. From 1716 foreign trade was opened up to private enterprise, and commerce across land frontiers – with Poland, the Ottoman Empire, China and Persia – was conducted with energy and confidence. Within Russia itself the demands of war produced some expanding markets and helped to develop the merchant class, a process which Peter deliberately encouraged. From 1711 he permitted internal free trade, and in 1719 the same rule was applied to iron mining and refining. By that time only two monopolies remained in state hands, and the government began to pay market prices for its supplies of metals. The trades in grain to feed the army, leather for harness and equipment, and flax and hemp for canvas sails and ropes were all modest success stories.

ACTIVITY 2.2

Draw up a table in two columns listing (a) positive economic change and (b) areas of continuity. On the whole, was the Russian economy changing or staying much the same?

Achievement

Peter's achievements in the economic sphere were at best uneven. By the end of his reign Russia was able to produce all kinds of military goods (cannon, small firearms, anchors), iron and copper, as well as vast quantities of sailcloth for the navy. However, despite Peter's late attempts to encourage private manufacturing and trade, the state was still the overwhelmingly dominant economic force. Moreover, the government's requirements were met less by economic expansion than by the ruthless exploitation of the pre-existing economy.

Orthodoxy and developments in the Church

Peter's personal position

Peter was an idiosyncratic but genuine believer:

- his formal education, such as it was, had been based in Orthodox tradition;
- he regularly not only attended but took an active part in church services;
- he believed in his own divine right to rule;
- he believed in his sacred duty to protect the Orthodox faith;
- in times of crisis he was borne up by a sense of being God's instrument;
- he built about 2000 churches;

However, as Anderson puts it, his belief 'lacked both psychological depth and intellectual subtlety'.[4] Along with his contempt for the externals of religion went an impatience with tradition and a lack of interest in the academic side of doctrine.

This did not make Peter particularly open-minded or tolerant. If from 1716 he relaxed the penalties for Old Believers, he compensated by doubling their taxes. He was an enemy of Judaism and had no intention of reversing Ivan the Terrible's expulsion of the Jews from Russia. Catholics in the conquered Baltic provinces were generally left alone, though Ukrainian Catholics and Uniates (Catholics who followed the Orthodox liturgy) were treated with great suspicion. Foreign Catholics were tolerated as long as they did not try to convert Russians or meddle in politics; but in 1719, suspicious of their close links to the Habsburg court in Vienna, Peter expelled the Jesuits altogether. He also approved of the forcible conversion of the Muslims and non-Orthodox Christians of the south and east. If anything, he seems to have been a strong defender of Orthodoxy.

How, then, to explain the near-blasphemous antics of the 'All-Joking, All-Drunken Synod'? At the end of the chapter, you'll find contrasting views put forward by Robert K. Massie and M.S. Anderson.

Attempts to increase the authority of the Tsar

Peter wanted the Church to be useful to the state and to Russian society. Of course, his own demands – those of the state and its wars – came first. After that, however, he saw the Church as responsible for education, poor relief and medical care. Unfortunately, at the beginning of the reign, and even in 1707, the reality was less inspiring. There were too many priests, and clerical marriage, combined with lack of regulation, had allowed the priesthood to become a hereditary caste. (It could not have escaped Peter's notice that, in contrast, in England, for example, although Anglican clergy could marry, preferment was ultimately in the hands of the supreme governor of the Church, the monarch.) Many priests were obsequious drunks, extremely poor and often wanderers without parishes. The numbers of monks were also becoming excessive, partly because men who entered monasteries were exempt from conscription. Clerical wealth was great and arguably excessive. Anderson points out that in 1700 about 557 monasteries and convents were supported by a total of 130 000 peasant households, while the Patriarch alone had nearly 9000. From 1701 until his death, therefore, Peter set about

- bringing the Church under increasing state control;
- diverting its wealth to finance wars and secular social projects.

Neither aim was entirely new but in these, as in other matters, Peter drove forward with ruthless energy and determination.

Milking the wealth of the Church

Peter saw no reason why the wealth of the Church should not be exploited as thoroughly as that of his other subjects.

These policies had a substantial impact: by 1710 the government had raised at least 1 million roubles in monastic taxation. However, Peter stopped well short of dissolving the monasteries and confiscating the Church's property. By 1722 about 20% of Russian peasants still laboured on Church lands.

Tightening state control

The financial arrangements were just one facet of Peter's intention to bring the Church wholly under state direction. In November 1708 he ordered it to anathematise (formally curse) Mazepa, the Ukrainian Cossack leader from whom Charles XII had hoped for support, on the grounds that he was a rebel and traitor. In 1716 the Tsar obliged new bishops to swear that they would not increase the numbers of clergy in their dioceses or build unnecessary churches. They should not allow monks to travel without written permission, should grant such permission only in exceptional cases and should not intervene in legal proceedings, except in cases of injustice.

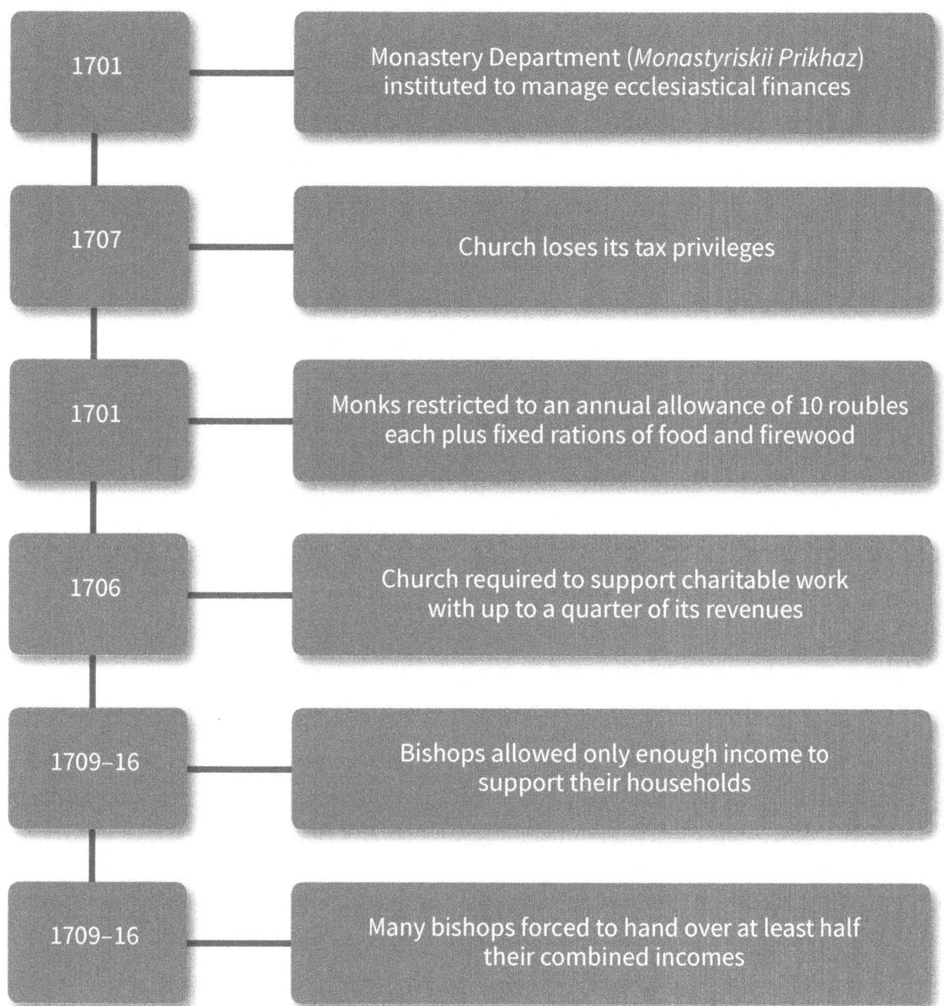

Figure 2.2: Peter's Church reforms

He now went further, by developing a coherent theory of absolutism, with the support of Feofan Prokopovich, the learned Archbishop of Novgorod. Prokopovich was very familiar with Western culture and had a great deal of sympathy with those forms of Protestantism which subordinated Church to state. From 1718 he produced learned writings on this theme, culminating in his 1722 *Right of the Monarchical Will*. Prokopovich argued that there was an original contract between people and ruler which put the Tsar above the law and entitled him, as Peter had claimed in 1721, to name his own successor. Drawing from the 17th-century English writer Thomas Hobbes, he emphasised that Peter's authority was that of 'every autocratic sovereign', implying that a Tsar's right did not rest upon Orthodoxy and was in no way exceptional.

Key term

Synod: a church council. In Russia, the government department which controlled the Church

The Most Holy Directing Synod, 1721

Upon this theoretical basis Peter constructed a machinery that reduced the Russian Church to an agency of government. The 1721 Spiritual Regulation established a new body first entitled the 'Spiritual College' but soon changed to 'Most Holy Directing Synod' to soothe traditionalist feelings. The **Synod** replaced the Patriarch and the occasional Church councils and had full authority over all spiritual matters and over Church property. Priests were required to report intended crimes they heard of in the confessional; to administer an oath of loyalty to townsmen and nobles; and to keep parish registers of births, marriages and deaths. The following year the Synod acquired an external lay supervisor, the Procurator-General *(Ober-Prokuror)*, who reported to the Tsar.

The consequences of state control

In this way, the Church became far more active in providing social services such as education, but parish priests were now servants of the state rather than carers of their flocks. This was radically different from the situation in the Catholic states of Europe, where the Church was an international body under the Pope. And even Protestant rulers such as George I of Great Britain did not reduce their national churches to departments of state. While in the long run Peter's reforms may have strengthened the Tsarist regime, they also turned ordinary people towards other spiritual outlets. In Anderson's words, 'Peter had won a victory, but in church affairs as elsewhere, at the cost of the psychological price which has to be paid when a highly traditional society breaks radically with its past.'[6]

Changes to central and local government

Two internal reforms

Between 1707 and his death in 1725, Peter continued his attempts to extend the authority of the state and to centralise control in his own hands. At first, with Charles XII marching on Moscow, these efforts were headlong and in response to events. But from about 1711, once the tide of the war with Sweden had begun to turn, his efforts became far more systematic. However, the greatest effort had to wait until after 1718, when the Tsar had recovered from a disastrous Turkish campaign, and victory over Sweden was at last assured. The new institutions he founded were all based on foreign models – the use of German titles for various offices was not accidental – and, for good or ill, gave Russia a system which lasted for almost 200 years. But it was not a Western-style autocracy based on the models of, for example, Prussia or France. Peter's Russia was based on the essentially Russian conception of the 'service state', where all citizens owed not merely allegiance but active service to the Tsar, and in which social status was tied to a man's ranking in the state's service.

Figure 2.3: Peter the Great in 1710. The French artist, Jean-Marc Nattier, follows a Western convention of using outdated armour to symbolise his warrior status

Central government

The *prikhazy* system of administration had to go. Filled with overlapping and conflicting jurisdictions, and without a coordinating organ now that the Boyar Council had disappeared, it was unfit for the purposes of fighting a long and exhausting modern war. Nor was it effective enough to enforce the authority of a Tsar who took his autocratic rights for granted, or to get an effective grip upon local government in the provinces.

The first important step was the creation in 1711 of the Senate, created on the same day that Russia declared war on the Turks. It was then essentially a regency council, empowered to act on the Tsar's behalf during his forthcoming absence on campaign, but in due course it became a permanent organ with very wide-ranging functions. Political administration and tax collection fell under its aegis, and it was also the highest court in the land. However, Peter tightly controlled its activities. In 1714, for example, he laid down procedures for preparing agendas for meetings and in 1716 he specified the frequency of meetings, hours of work and a scale of fines for unauthorised absence or carelessness. If Peter hoped to make the most of the imperfect material available to him by such bullying he failed: one of the original nine senators was illiterate and two more were prosecuted for corruption. Yet the Senate was to survive as a supreme court until the collapse of Tsardom itself.

Key terms

Fiskals: secret administrative policemen charged with spying

College: a committee of officials and ministers, based on the German, Danish and Swedish systems

Gubernii: eight administrative areas into which Russia was divided in 1708. Another three were added in 1713–14

Corruption was tackled from 1711 by a set of secret administrative policemen, the **fiskals**, charged with 'secretly spying on all things'. The problem here was essentially the same as that with the Senate, and indeed at every level of government: there simply were not enough honest and effective civil servants to make the system work. The loathed *fiskals* were soon notorious for their own greed and misuse of power.

Far more successful were the 11 administrative **Colleges** set up from 1718, after at least three years of research and preparation. Based on German, Danish and Swedish models, the Colleges were committees of eight to ten officials and ministers working under a president and vice-president. Given that Peter's priorities were always war and diplomacy, it is hardly surprising that from the first, the three dealing with foreign affairs, the army and the navy were treated as the most important. Three of the others dealt with different aspects of finance, industry and business; one dealt with internal affairs such as law and order; and one dealt with the landowners. As each College managed a specified area of government, over the whole of Russia many of the confusing overlaps and contradictions of the *prikhazy* system were eliminated, and the Senate was able to focus upon general policy and its work as a court. Of course, there remained the problem of finding properly educated and reliable people to make the new system work. However, it was unquestionably a much more systematic and rational extension of government than any of the Tsar's earlier reforms.

In 1721 Peter took a further step along this road to effective close regulation by creating the post of Procurator-General *(Generalprokuror).* This official was to supervise the Senate, the *fiskals* and the Colleges, making him effectively head of the whole Russian civil service and almost as powerful as Prince Alexander Danilovich Menshikov, one of the dominating political figures of Peter's reign. In 1722 the Tsar added a kind of ombudsman, the *Reketmeister*, to investigate complaints about the behaviour and decisions of the Colleges.

Local government

Early attempts to reform provincial government were no more successful. In 1708 Russia was divided into eight huge administrative areas called **gubernii**, to which another three were added in 1713–14. Each *guberniya* was given a governor and vice-governor with authority over all aspects of military and civil administration. Their officials were often given strikingly foreign titles: the *ober-kommandant*, for example, ran military affairs.

Key terms

Uezdy: districts which were subdivisions of gubernii. The divisions were traditionally based on natural boundaries

Doli: districts which were subdivisions of gubernii. The divisions were not based on natural boundaries but on population – the doli were drawn up in 1715 to contain precisely 5536 tax-paying households

ACTIVITY 2.3

Class discussion: how far were Peter's civil and military reforms hampered by lack of able and honest personnel?

Gubernii were subdivided into provinces, and the provinces, at first, into **uezdy** (districts), which on the whole were based on traditional natural boundaries. In 1715 the *uezdy* were abolished in favour of ***doli***, artificial districts supposed to contain precisely 5536 tax-paying households. The result was confusion and disaffection. Like the French revolutionaries 80 years later, Peter's instinct was not to adapt the old systems to new purposes, but to sweep them ruthlessly away.

The reform of the army

Until 1716 Peter's military efforts continued to focus upon measures for winning the wars against the Swedes and the Turks, the most important of which remained mass conscription. From at least 1709 the rigorous drilling of the infantry attracted the admiration of foreign observers, who rated it as good as any in Europe. The weak point was still the quality of the officers, a significant number of whom were foreigners, a problem which Anderson contends was never really solved throughout the Tsarist period.

There were, however, a number of measures designed to reduce the army's dependence upon foreign expertise. One way was to sack incompetents: after the humiliating defeat by the Turks on the River Pruth in 1711, Peter dismissed no fewer than 56 foreign officers, including five generals. The other side of the coin was to train experts at home by creating training schools. To the artillery school he had already established in Moscow, the Tsar added schools of engineering in Moscow (1709) and St Petersburg (1719).

The first step towards a systematic reform of the army was the Military Regulation of 1716, which laid down a comprehensive organisation for the whole army. It was followed by the creation in 1719 of the War College to replace the old war chancery and artillery *prikhaz*, thus providing for the first time a centralised administrative body closely controlled by the Tsar.

There were similar efforts to reform the navy. In 1718 a Naval Academy was opened in St Petersburg as a kind of practical finishing school for graduates of the school of navigation opened the same year in Moscow. However, because the technical demands of the maritime service were so much greater than in the army, the Russian navy remained heavily dependent upon foreign officers and shipwrights. Even at the end of the reign most warships built in Russia were the work of British builders.

Voices from the past

Alexander Menshikov, 1673–1729

Menshikov came of obscure but probably minor gentry origins. Taken into the service of Peter's favourite Lefort, he quickly caught Peter's eye. After service in the Azov campaigns of 1695–96, he accompanied the Tsar on his great embassy to the West and worked alongside him in Dutch shipyards. After Lefort's death he became Peter's principal adviser and a committed supporter of the Tsar's reforms. Upon Peter's death in 1725, he helped to ensure that Peter was succeeded by his reform-minded widow, Catherine. Under Catherine (1725–1727) he exercised enormous power, and on her death was instrumental in enthroning Peter's grandson as Peter II. He was now ruler of Russia in all but name. However, his attempt to establish his family's power permanently by marrying his daughter to the Tsar led to his overthrow by members of the old nobility. Exiled to Siberia, he died there in 1729.

The Introduction of the Table of Ranks and the Service State

The **Table of Ranks** represents, perhaps, Peter's most ambitious move to produce a rationalised and systematised bureaucracy by extending the Russian tradition of a service nobility. There were three hierarchies of service: military and naval, civil and court. The military column was subdivided into four: infantry, guards, artillery and navy. The columns were divided horizontally into 14 grades. Thus as a man rose in his particular service, from lieutenant to colonel say, so he rose through these 14 grades of nobility. Those in the military and naval services, and the more senior civil servants, were ranked with the highest of the old nobility, and guards were set two grades higher than the others. Advancement was to be by a combination of merit and length of service, reinforcing the notion that high rank was not a natural perquisite of noble birth.

Key term

Table of Ranks: a system, introduced by Peter I, of making rank in the nobility dependent upon rank in the military or civil service

ACTIVITY 2.4

Construct a chart showing the reformed structure of Russian central and local government by 1725.

However, this was not a deliberate attempt to push the old nobility aside with the creation of a new elite. It was assumed that recruits into the service nobility would continue to come largely from the landowning class, which was why the lowest ranks of the civil administration – clerks, for example – did not appear in the Table at all. However, such a process did gradually emerge. The last creation of a boyar was made as early as 1709 and Western titles such as count and baron were on their way in.

Peter was prepared to promote non-nobles when he had to but, however hard he tried, he could never find civilians of the right quality. That meant that he increasingly had to employ the army to carry out tasks of civil administration that went beyond mere policing. By 1725 there were commissioned and non-commissioned officers in senior positions in every civil department, taking part in tax collection and census-taking and even judicial work. In 1717 a special military tribunal was set up to investigate corruption in the Senate.

Thus by 1725 the 'service state' was emerging as a massive bureaucracy, more coherently organised than ever before, but existing side by side and in conjunction with the old landowning nobility. However, in no way did the organs of administration enjoy institutional autonomy or play any significant role in the formulation of policy. That was Peter's sphere, and as long as he lived he kept the Colleges and Senate under strict and close supervision.

Social developments, Westernisation and the extent of change by 1725

While the beginnings of the service state had introduced the complexity of a new elite, the complex overall structure of Russia society was simplified by the soul tax.

Social developments

Did Peter have a social policy?

It was once argued that Peter the Great had no social policy at all, in that he was not interested in changing the basic social structure. Historians still accept that verdict but with qualifications. For example, by 1705 he had largely succeeded in enforcing the wearing of Western clothes by merchants and nobles in towns. That, and attempts to introduce a measure of health care and poor relief, were superficial changes. His main goal was to make all social classes more heavily dependent on the state, to which all other social changes were subsidiary.

The nobility

The nobility were not a single class but a bewildering variety of groups, ranging from the 15 greatest old boyar families to relatively poor provincial nobles whose way of life hardly differed from that of the peasants around them. The soul tax instituted in 1724, by simplifying classifications for tax purposes, also simplified social structures. For example, those in the lowest-ranking group of single-household gentry, the *odnodvortsy*, were reclassified as peasants. However, this reform could not take effect until long after Peter was dead.

How far did he succeed in creating a new elite compelled to serve the state? A 1714 law on inheritance, which forbade the splitting of estates between sons, was intended to force more nobles into state service. It provoked so much resistance that it was withdrawn in 1731 – but nobles often found themselves dependent on the salaries and prestige which only state service could provide. While the Table of Ranks was aimed at linking noble rank to service, it did not deprive the old nobility of their titles, irrespective of service. Recruits into the service nobility almost always came from the existing nobility, so the creation of a new elite overlapped with the continuation of the old aristocracy.

The peasantry

Professor Simon Dixon points out that, because of a lack of sources, we still do not know very much about the conditions of peasants on the smaller Russian estates, and that regional differences have often been underemphasised. We certainly have almost no evidence of the ideas and motives which drove members of this almost wholly illiterate population. Even so, we can still make some useful generalisations.

It is clear that serfdom was extended and strengthened. Ascription and the purchase of villages by commercial concerns did much to spread serfdom into industry. The soul tax of 1724 made nobles responsible for their serfs' payments and thereby gave them even greater authority over them.

Key term

Three-field system: a system (which had also been practised in medieval England) in which two fields were planted with different crops, while a third one was left unused, or 'fallow'. This cyclically allowed each field one year off in three and helped avoid exhausting the soil through over-farming.

The Petrine period saw the emergence of multiple-family households, especially in areas where farmland land was plentiful and fertile, and labour therefore scarce. Even more important, Dixon argues, were the increasing burdens imposed by the state. From 1679 taxation was based on the household rather than on land, making it difficult for small households to survive and discouraging adult sons from setting up on their own. By 1725 households on many large estates contained eight or nine males, far larger than was common in the West.

The commune or *mir* also encouraged collective decision-making, limited the scope for individual initiative and reinforced conservatism. Governed by an assembly of elected elders, the *mir* governed the timing of ploughing, sowing and harvesting, oversaw the sharing of ploughs, collected taxes and maintained law and order. Crucially, it regularly redistributed land according to the changing needs of each household, ensuring that everyone could be fed but working against the development of large holdings. Adherence to the use of a **three-field system** of **strip farming** reinforced this communal land-management system to ensure that there could be no **agricultural revolution** in Russia.

The soul tax introduced in 1724 not only reinforced the tendency to large households and communal decision-making, but encouraged the simplification of peasant society. Before the tax was introduced about 10% of the peasant population were slaves *(kholopy)*, who were not subject to taxation. By classifying peasants as taxpayers – and therefore as serfs rather than slaves – the system actually brought about the demise of the *kholopy* class. They were not replaced because there were more serfs available, and because very poor peasants who might otherwise have become slaves were sheltered in the large households. At the other end of the scale, the poorest of the noble groups were classified as peasants. By 1719 55.8% of the whole peasant population were serfs, and in the central, longest-settled regions the proportion was much higher. The rest were 'state' peasants, bound to no particular landlord but owing taxes and labour services. Arguably, therefore, almost the entire peasant population was enserfed.

Key terms

Strip farming: this system allotted villagers small parcels of land in each of the three fields. It was fair in that it ensured that everyone had a share of the better and worse land. It was also inefficient, since everyone's land was scattered in pieces, thus reducing yield.

Agricultural revolution: a rapid change in farming methods resulting in higher productivity. Britain had an agricultural revolution during the 18th century. Unemployed labourers then moved to cities where many found work in the growing number of factories, thus feeding the industrial revolution.

Polarity: a situation in which two sets of ideas or groups are completely opposed to each other. It suggests that there is little or no middle ground.

Westernisation?

On the surface the elite – the nobility and the wealthier town-dwellers – had become Westernised. In urban areas, beards and traditional clothing such as the long kaftan looked very old-fashioned. Their diet was changing too, in favour of wine rather than spirits, sugar to replace honey, and other delicacies. Education was expanding. By contrast, the bulk of the population was still steeped in traditional peasant culture. Old Believers clung to the old religious ways and serfdom, far from vanishing, was extended and strengthened.

However, as Dixon points out, that apparent **polarity** disguises quite deep differences within the elite. We have already seen a growing rivalry between the new service nobility, represented by Alexander Menshikov, and more traditionally minded nobles like Prince Vasily Dolgoruky. It is possible to argue that a superficial cultural Westernisation covered deeply ingrained, very Russian attitudes.

Opposition

Astrakhan

We have already seen that resistance to Peter's government was widespread, ranging from passive disobedience to conspiracy and warfare. One low-level form was direct disobedience to orders that were hard to enforce, such as continuing to build Russian-style river boats. Two more, very common among the peasants,

Hidden voices

Mass flight of the Russian peasantry

Because peasants were almost all illiterate they left no records of their own, so we have to explain their behaviour through the observations of others.

Use the material in this section and elsewhere in the chapter to identify the reasons why so many fled to the frontier regions. Arrange these factors in order of importance, ensuring that you have evidence to support your choice.

were rural banditry and mass flight to the periphery. Flight contributed to a third type of resistance – armed rebellion. There were three great frontier revolts:

1. That in Astrakhan, discussed in the previous chapter;
2. One among the semi-nomadic Bashkir of the northern steppe;
3. Most dangerously of all, by the Don Cossacks under Kondraty Bulavin.

Key term

Tsarevitch: a Tsar's son. Later practice limited the term to the oldest son, the heir to the throne.

However, none of these was directed personally at the Tsar or had any clear programme beyond the removal of specific local grievances. None of them came near to threatening the Russian heartland and none was ultimately able to stand up to strong forces of regular troops.

In Astrakhan, as we have seen, the eruption was caused by a combination of Streltsy discontent, Old Believer suspicions, migrant and criminal fugitive elements, and rumours that the real Tsar had been overthrown. While the rebels rapidly took Astrakhan and two other towns, they failed to stir the Don Cossacks; when powerful government forces arrived they were rapidly defeated. Far more serious from Peter's perspective was the opposition coalescing around the heir to the throne, **Tsarevich** Alexis.

The Bashkir were a non-Russian Muslim people inhabiting the northern edge of the steppe between the River Volga and the Urals. Herders of goats, cattle and camels, these highly mobile and skilled horse archers had long harassed and slowed the Russian advance. In the mid-16th century they became subjects of the Tsar but the encroachment of Russian settlements on their pastures produced revolts in 1662–1664 and 1675–1683. By 1707 the combination of advancing Russian settlers and the depredations of Peter's tax collectors had become intolerable. Early in 1708, while Peter was facing Charles XII's advance on Moscow, they rose once again in revolt.

Burning Russian villages in the valleys of the Ufa and Kama rivers, Bashkir raiders advanced dangerously close to the city of Kazan. Peter could spare only three regular regiments to deal with them, and even they soon had to be withdrawn to face the Swedes. But that expedition was enough to divide the loosely organised Bashkir: while the eastern bands continued their devastating raids unmolested, the western Bashkir prudently submitted. Nor did the revolt spread to other steppe peoples. Peter's government was even able to persuade another people, the Kalmyks of the open steppe to the south-west, to provide the government with 10 000 irregulars. (The Kalmyks were not Russian, but significantly they were also not Turkic-speaking and not Muslim, but Buddhist and of Mongol descent.)

With that the revolt, with its loose organisation and divided leadership, was doomed. However, the rebellion had demonstrated the underlying weakness of Moscow's grip on the fringe areas. The Bashkir were still formidable, as we shall see later.

Don Cossacks

The Don Cossack revolt was also a consequence of the overreaching centralisation of the state. However, their rising won the support of a far wider range of malcontents, and therefore had the potential to develop into an upheaval as

Speak like a historian

The Marxists

The 19th-century political and economist theorist, Karl Marx, argued that all states pass through the same stages of development, but at different times and at different speeds. He argued that all such change is about economic conflict between the dominant classes and those on the rise. Thus emperors, kings and nobles will be overthrown by a rising industrial middle class, the **bourgeoisie**, and the bourgeoisie will in turn be overthrown by the industrial working class, the *proletariat*.

Marxist interpretations of history were most strongly in favour in the middle decades of the 20th century. Much of this work has proved very illuminating but Marxist versions have been powerfully challenged by *revisionists*. Marxist historians used to argue that Peter's encouragement of private enterprise produced the Russian 'bourgeoisie' – but the more one looks for that class the harder it is to find. We have already seen that the merchant class in Russia was timid, and dependent upon state initiatives, while the towns in which they lived had no real powers of self-government. Numerically, that class was minuscule. Of a population of almost 16 million in 1719 no more than 600 000 were town-dwellers; and of those most were peasants and the main urban activity was, curiously, agriculture. Class lines were very blurred. In 1721 town-dwelling managers or owners of industrial enterprises were permitted to own serfs, and younger sons of nobles were pressed towards trades and professions, thus blurring the distinction between themselves and the gentry.

Key terms

Bourgeoisie: French term originally meaning 'towndwellers'. In Marxist discourse it has come to mean 'industrialurban middle class'

Ataman: a Cossack leader.

ACTIVITY 2.5

Draw up a table in two columns and list evidence which supports and contradicts the idea that Peter's reign saw the rise of a thriving, confident industrial middle class.

dangerous as that of Pugachev (for which see Chapter 4) over 70 years later. A successful rising here could cut off the vital southern military and naval bases by which Peter set such store. As we saw in Chapter 1, the stationing of discontented Streltsy in this region only added to the inflammable mix.

The relatively empty lands of western Ukraine had attracted large numbers of fugitives: serfs fleeing Peter's exaction, runaway conscripts and deserters from the huge drafts of forced labourers bound for Veronezh, Taganrog and Azov. The Cossacks sheltered these people, and demands for their return usually remained unanswered. Peter's attempt to recover the fugitives by force was the immediate cause of the uprising.

In September 1707 Prince Yuri Dolgoruky appeared on the River Don with 1200 regular soldiers at his back to demand the return of the deserters. Like the Bashkir, the Don Cossacks were divided, some frightened by Dolgoruky's show of force, others determined to fight. One **ataman**, Lukyan Maximov, offered to cooperate with the Russians, but another, Kondraty Bulavin, had other ideas. On the night of 9 October 1707 he surprised the Russians' camp and wiped them out. But Bulavin had no clear goals apart from opposition to reform and reformers. He was fighting, he said, not against the Tsar but against the criminals, 'Germans' and religious innovators who surrounded him.

Key term

Internal exile: exile is a punishment in which someone is sent to a foreign country to live. Russia being so large, and with an extensive empire, people could be sent into internal exile, forced to live far from their own home, usually in some part of the Asian empire, at a considerable distance from the Russian-speaking part west of the Urals.

Maximov, realising that only prompt action could deflect Peter's anger, raised his own army and defeated Bulavin, afterwards mutilating and shooting all his prisoners. But Bulavin was far from finished. He raised a new army and defeated Maximov in battle in April 1708. His raiders burnt settlements as far north as Tula, provoking the fear that he would attack Moscow just as Charles XII advanced from the west. Charles's decision to rest his army for three months near Minsk relieved that danger, but the threat to the Lower Don bases was such that Peter considered going there to take command himself. In the end he did not go but sent Prince Yury's brother, Prince Vasily Dolgoruky, with 10 000 regulars.

Meanwhile, Bulavin again defeated (and this time captured and executed) Maximov, and unsuccessfully attacked Azov. However, that failure, combined with Dolgoruky's advance, swung most Cossacks once again behind the peace faction. Bulavin compounded the problem by dividing his army into three, allowing Dolgoruky to defeat the detachments in detail. Bulavin, seeing that further resistance was hopeless, committed suicide, and in November Dolgoruky brought the remaining rebels to battle, killing 3000 of them. The rebellion was over, an

Voices from the past

Prince Vasily Vladimirovich Dolgoruky, c.1667–1746

Figure 2.4: Vasily Vladimirovich Dolgoruky

From an old boyar family, Dolgoruky was one of Peter's oldest associates. In 1685 he entered the Tsar's court as a *stolnik*, a privileged servant, and in 1700 he joined the Preobrazhensky Regiment. He served with distinction in the early years of the Swedish war before being posted to Ukraine in 1706, where he took a leading role in defeating Bulavin. He had a cavalry command at the Battle of Poltava, served as an emissary to Poland in 1715 and accompanied Peter on his second visit to the West in 1717–18. Up to this point Peter regarded him as one of his most capable and trustworthy servants.

However, Dolgoruky was one of the circle of nobles who disliked Peter's reforms, sympathised with his more conservative son Alexis, and hoped for an early succession. After Alexis's death in prison in 1718 he seems to have protested to Peter about his treatment of the Tsarevich. Accused of conspiracy, he was sentenced to **internal exile**.

When in 1725 Peter's second wife, Catherine I, succeeded to the throne, Dolgoruky was restored to favour and promoted. He served as commander in the Caucasus from 1726 and two years later was made Field Marshal and a privy councillor. He supported the succession in 1730 of Peter the Great's niece Anna and was instrumental in imposing upon her conditions designed to limit her power. She made him a Senator and president of the War College, but repudiated the conditions next year. Dolgoruky was dismissed, imprisoned for eight years and then exiled to the Solovetsky Monastery on an island in the White Sea. Freed in 1741 by Anna's successor, Elizabeth, he was restored to the presidency of the War College, where he made a number of improvements to the Russian army before his death in 1746.

ending signalled by the hanging of 200 men on rafts which were afterwards allowed to drift down the river past the Cossack settlements.

Tsarevich Alexis

Background and character

Alexis, born in February 1690, was Peter's only surviving son by his first wife, Evdokia, whom he later divorced. Separated from his mother at the age of eight to be brought up by his paternal aunt Natalia, force-fed a formidable Germanic educational diet and in any case no scholar, the Tsarevich had a miserable childhood. He became 'timid, secretive and lacking in self-confidence' but nevertheless capable of extreme obstinacy.[7] For comfort he turned to drink and to the externals of the Orthodox religion, especially to ritual and fasts, and preferred to have priests about him at all times. By 1707 he had become a focus for those at court who either rejected or disliked the pace of the reforms. Although Alexis was totally unsuited to the role of future Tsar, Peter was determined that his son should share the burdens of government and his own vision for Russia.

Under these circumstances the question is not why there was a conflict between father and son, but whether Peter's minister Menshikov deliberately fostered their animosity. There is evidence that Menshikov systematically bullied Alexis in order to retain his own position.

By 1707 Peter was greatly dissatisfied with his son but he did not give up easily. He put Alexis in charge of important administrative tasks in Moscow and Smolensk and later transferred him to the shipbuilding programme on Lake Ladoga. In both instances Alexis proved neither interested nor capable. In 1711 Peter ordered Alexis to marry a foreign Protestant, Charlotte of Brunswick-Wolfenbüttel, as part of his drive to extend Russian influence and Romanov prestige in Germany. The Tsarevich, now a religious conservative, resented a match which did not even require his bride to become Orthodox. Even more disappointingly for Peter, he had not the slightest interest in military affairs in general and cared nothing for the Swedish war in particular.

By 1716 Alexis was a key symbol of resistance, at the very time that Peter's health began to deteriorate sharply. Those who wished to reverse the Petrine reforms – the Dolgoruky family prominent among them – pinned their hopes on an early death and a smooth succession. But Alexis was not the man to lead a strong reversionary interest, and certainly not one to engineer a coup should Peter's life be unexpectedly prolonged. Instead, he became terrified of a violent response by his father, panicked and fled to Vienna with his mistress. The Holy Roman Emperor, Charles VI, and his ministers were thrown into a quandary: they could not ignore the hysterical young man, who might indeed be useful to them, but at the same time they could not afford to alienate Peter. There was concern that Russian troops might invade the Austrian province of Silesia or even Bohemia (the modern Czech Republic). Charles therefore settled for protecting Alexis without officially acknowledging his presence, hiding him elsewhere in his empire, first in a castle in the Tyrol and then in Italy.

Peter could not ignore this embarrassing situation, which threatened both his own and Russian prestige, at the very moment that a dispute over the Russian presence in the German state of Mecklenburg soured relations with Austria. His solution was both devious and characteristically ruthless. He sent an emissary, Peter Tolstoy, to entice Alexis back to Russia at any cost. A promise of forgiveness and a quiet life combined with threats – the Austrians would soon stop protecting him, Peter himself would come to Italy to get him, he would be separated from his mistress – were enough to break the man's resistance. Just for good measure, when the Austrian officials tried to ask Alexis if he was really returning of his own free will, Tolstoy's entourage made such a tight circle around him that conversation was impossible.

Alexis arrived back in Moscow in February 1717. He readily gave up his claim to the succession, and Peter's son, by Catherine, his second wife, was declared heir to the throne. But that did not, of course, remove the basic problem. Alexis was still a focus for discontent and could at any moment renew his claim. And if that happened and he became Tsar, Peter's reforms and all the men associated with them, Menshikov included, would be swept aside. Unrest, revolt, a palace coup or even civil war seemed more than possible. There were many powerful figures who shared Peter's view that Alexis would be a threat as long as he remained alive.

In March 1718 Peter therefore set up the Secret Chancellery, an agency under Tolstoy's leadership empowered to investigate the suspected conspiracy. Despite the free use of torture and Alexis's anxiety to throw suspicion onto his friends, the inquisitors could find no solid evidence until they interrogated his mistress, Alfrosinia. Under pressure she claimed that her lover had never wanted to renounce the succession and that he intended to abolish the navy, reduce the army to a defence force and turn his back on St Petersburg. Under torture Alexis himself admitted having been promised Austrian military aid: a claim which was almost certainly false. Nevertheless, Peter got his conviction: on 3 July a special assembly of 126 nobles recommended the death sentence; four days later Alexis suddenly died in custody. Officially he had suffered a massive stroke but the real cause of death has never been ascertained.

The demise of Alexis and the eight executions which followed seemed to remove the immediate threat, real or imagined, in the heart of government, but it did not quash more distant resistance. Mass flights of peasants at once became more common and larger in scale, a tendency accentuated by poor harvests in 1722,

Voices from the Past

Peter Tolstoy, 1645–1729

Tolstoy was one of Peter I's ablest diplomats. Already a courtier when the reign began, in 1697 he was dispatched to Venice to learn Italian and shipbuilding. In 1701 he became Russia's first ambassador to Constantinople, where he worked to keep the Turks and Swedes apart. Imprisoned there when the Turks declared war on Russia in 1710, he returned home in 1714 to become a Senator and an ally of Alexander Menshikov. His conduct of his mission to Naples in 1717 and his subsequent presidency of the Secret Chancellery illustrate his ability and ruthlessness. On Peter's death he supported Menshikov in securing the succession of Peter's second wife, Catherine. However, at Catherine's death in 1727 he fell out with Menshikov and was exiled to the Solovetsky Monastery, where he died in 1729.

1723 and 1724. Localised and minor acts of violence became far more frequent. The *Preobrazhensky Prikhaz* heard 91 such cases in 1718 but 448 in 1724. Peter had secured the Russian state but at the cost of increased popular opposition.

Foreign affairs and wars

War with Sweden

Charles XII probably aimed to dethrone Peter, get rid of his imported foreign experts and impose a crushing indemnity. At first it seemed that nothing could stop him, especially as the Don Cossack revolt led by Bulavin broke out at the same time. Peter sensibly avoided battle and fell back before the Swedish advance, but he pursued a scorched-earth policy to ensure that Charles would find no supplies or shelter of any kind. Towns and villages were to be evacuated and burnt, crops destroyed, livestock removed, threshing floors and millstones broken, bridges wrecked, forests cut down. This certainly slowed the Swedes but it did not stop them. Moscow itself would have been in danger had not Charles decided to turn south into Ukraine.

The lack of supplies was certainly one factor in his thinking, as was Ukraine's reported abundance of food and lack of strong Russian garrisons. He also hoped to link up with Mazepa, **hetman** of the Cossacks there, who had promised him 20 000 men. Mazepa was not pro-Swedish but wished to maintain his own autonomy by playing Russians, Swedes, Poles and Turks off against each other. His own followers complained about the hardships of service with the Russian army, including physical abuse. Most importantly, Peter had refused to provide adequate troops to defend Ukraine. So Mazepa turned to the Swedes for protection.

However, Charles's decision was fatal. Before he could reach Ukraine local Russian forces had wrought such havoc in the Cossack settlements that only 3000 or 4000 eventually joined Mazepa. Ukrainians, unimpressed by the prospect of renewed Polish Catholic rule backed by Swedish arms, launched guerrilla attacks against Charles's advancing forces. The winter of 1708–09 was the worst in living memory and hundreds of Swedes died or were maimed by exposure. One of their chaplains wrote of 'men without hands, others without hands or feet, others deprived of fingers, face, ears and noses, others crawling like quadrupeds'.[8]

Charles relied upon drawing the Russians into a pitched battle, of repeating Narva. But Peter and his principal southern general, Menshikov, refused to engage in a major battle, wearing the Swedes down with minor skirmishes and long marches. On top of that, the hoped-for Turkish and Crimean support was not forthcoming. Thus as the Swedes marched further from reinforcements and supplies, they found little food and almost no allies. Their numbers steadily thinned and they faced exhaustion.

ACTIVITY 2.6

Using material from this and the previous chapter, first plan and then write an answer to the following essay question:

'Peter I's regime was never threatened by internal resistance.' How far do you agree with this assessment?

Key term

Hetman: a Ukrainian leader.

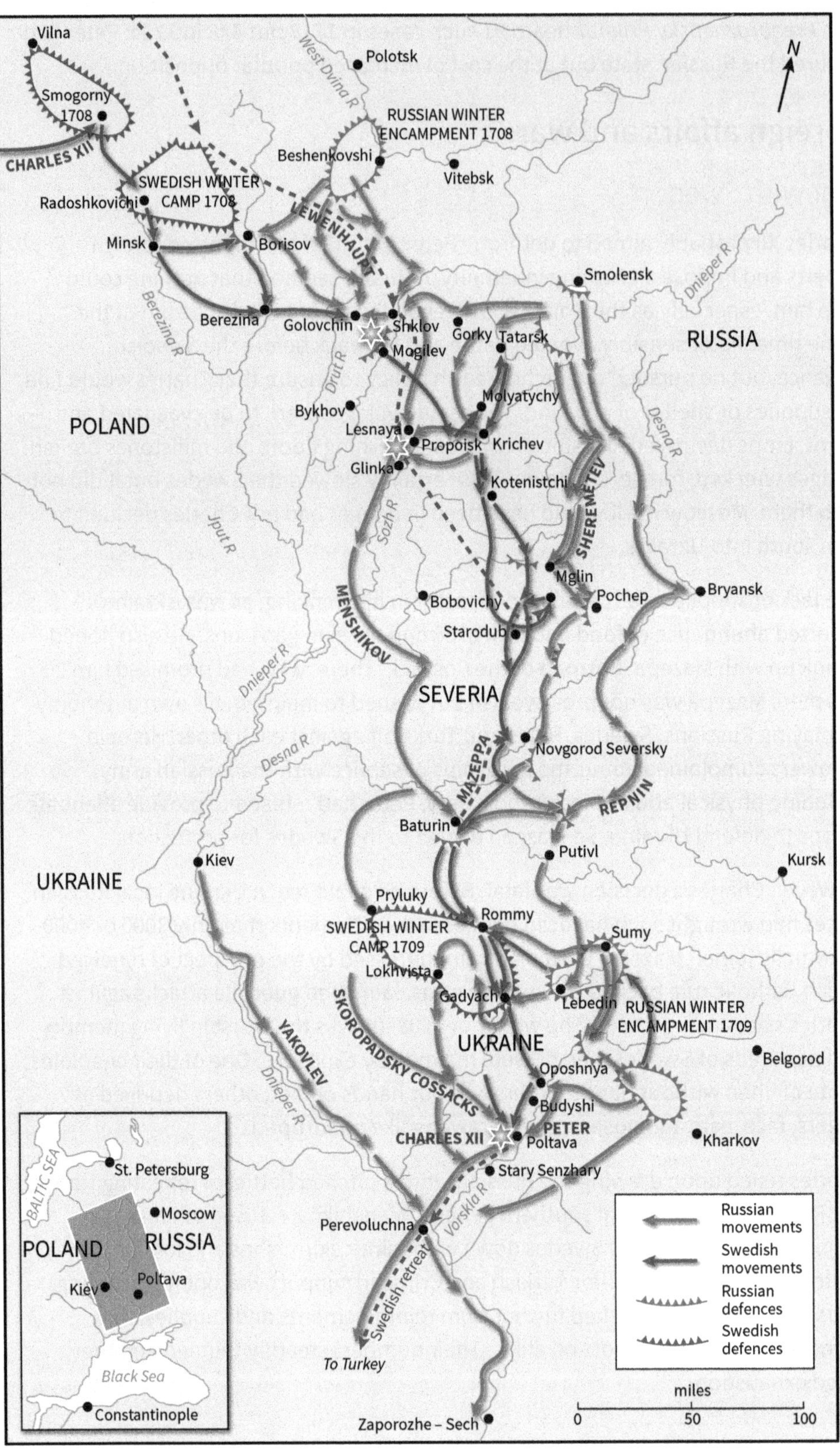

Figure 2.5: The Swedish invasion of Russia

The Battle of Poltava

By the time that the Swedes reached Poltava, Charles had been wounded in the foot and his two principal generals had quarrelled. He had no more than 20 000 men remaining and possibly significantly less, while Peter had up to 45 000 troops. Why, then, did Charles accept battle? Probably he saw that his only chance was to fight a decisive battle as soon as possible, before his strength was eroded any further. He may also have expected the Russians to do as they had done so often before: engage briefly and then rapidly retreat. Charles thus banked on a swift cavalry-led breakthrough and wrongly assumed that the Russians' escape route could be easily blocked. That led him into two more fatal errors: he failed to deploy his artillery and he detached a large force to cut off the Russians' line of retreat. But this time Peter was determined to fight a decisive action and, thanks to his military reforms, his men were no longer the rabble of Narva. The Swedes were mown down by Peter's 102 guns and the steady fire of his disciplined infantry, while their own firepower was weakened by inferior gunpowder. According to the official Russian records, the Swedes lost 6901 dead and wounded, with another 2760 taken prisoner. Russian casualties were 1345 killed and 3290 wounded. Three days later, the remnants of the once-terrifying Swedish army surrendered at Perevolochna on the River Dneiper, while Charles and a few hundred cavalry escaped across the river into Turkish territory.

Russian historians used to argue that after Poltava Peter was in control of events. He was able to restore and sustain Augustus in Poland and to conclude treaties with Denmark and with Frederick I of Prussia. Britain offered to mediate between Russian and Sweden; and the French were willing to let Prussia mediate between themselves and the Grand Alliance of Britain, Austria and the Dutch.

However, as Lindsey Hughes points out, at the time even Peter did not expect an early peace. Charles was not about to give up and was urging the Turks to intervene. Peter was enormously relieved when, early in 1710, the Sultan agreed to renew an existing truce; and even then he could not be sure that the peace would hold. In the north, Britain, France and the Dutch Republic were not prepared to let Russia replace Sweden's dominance in the Baltic. Peter's own agreements with other Baltic powers prevented him eliminating a pocket of 8000 Swedish troops in Pomerania and he was too short of cash to subsidise the Danish fleet. St Petersburg was not safe until June 1710, when the Russians captured Viborg in Finland, and not until the end of the year did Peter secure the Baltic coasts, including Riga and Tallinn. Even then he took care to conciliate his new Baltic subjects by guaranteeing their liberties, privileges, religion and laws. On the face of it, a new war was the very thing he could least afford.

ACTIVITY 2.7

Identify the causes of the Swedish failure at Poltava and organise them into three groups: long-term factors, short-term factors and immediate factors. Which seem to you to be the most important? Prepare an argument supporting your case for class discussion.

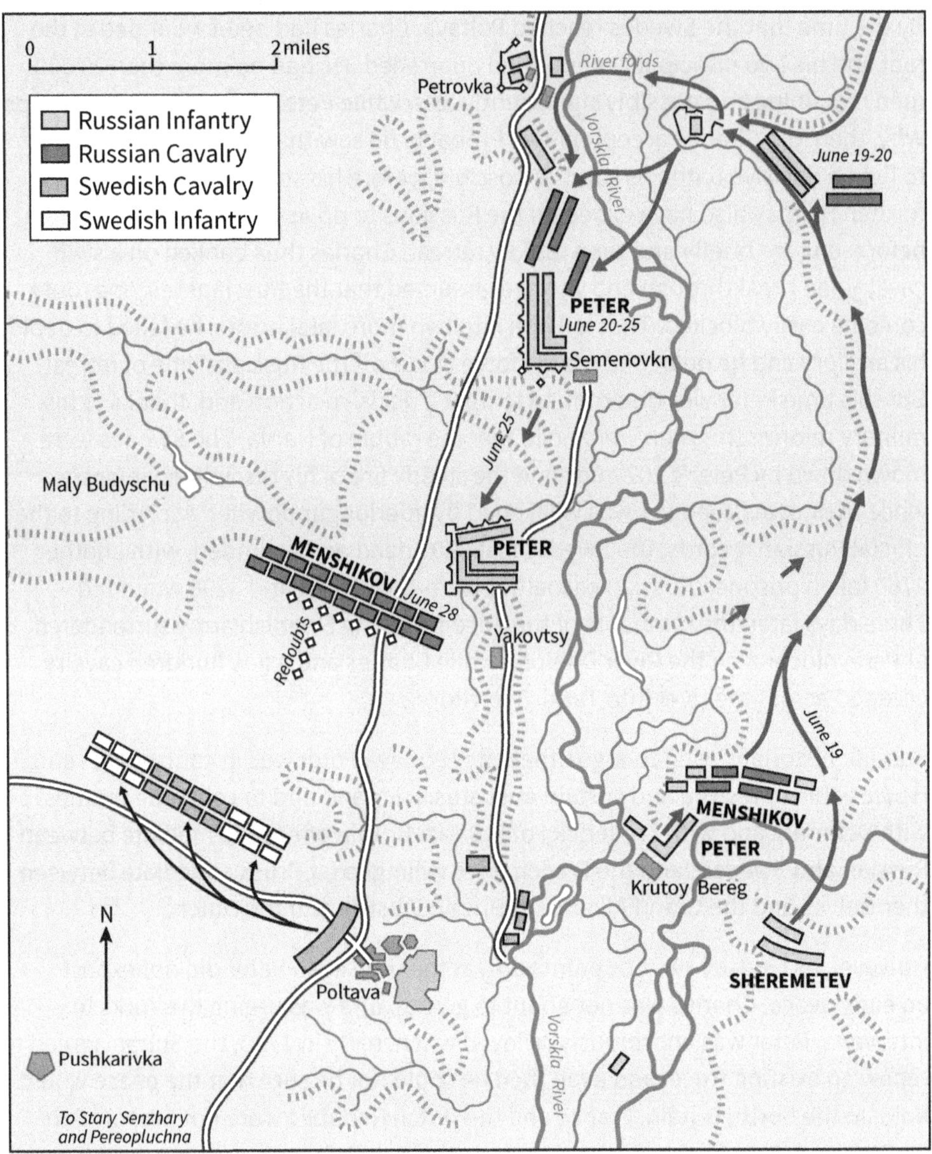

Figure 2.6: The Battle of Poltava

Figure 2.7: Pierre-Denis Marten's *Battle of Poltava*

War with Turkey

Why did the Turks declare war in November 1711?

- Charles had been pressing the Turks to declare war on Peter.
- The Turks were irritated by Peter's demands to hand over Charles XII.
- The rabidly anti-Russian Crimean khan, Devlet-Girei, offered Tartar troops to escort Charles north, and succeeded in winning the Sultan's ear.
- French diplomacy, loans to Charles by British bankers, Austrian neutrality and even the intervention of the Sultan's doctor and mother all influenced the Ottoman decision to go to war.
- The expansion of Russian influence in Ukraine was particularly unwelcome to the Ottomans.

Historians have generally argued that Peter's main objective was always his Baltic 'window on the West' and that the Turkish declaration of war was an unwelcome distraction. However, it can be argued that Peter thought the south to be at least equally important and was perfectly willing to fight a major campaign there.

Disaster on the Pruth July 1711

Peter abandoned his usual caution in favour of speed and allowed his troops to outstrip his supply trains. He expected assistance from Christian revolts but the key provinces of Moldavia and Wallachia (in modern Romania and Moldova) did not move. The only Balkan Christians to rebel against the Turks were the Serbs and Montenegrins, peoples far too distant to be of any use to Peter's campaign. Moreover, Russian forces were hopelessly outnumbered. The Ottoman Empire possessed a population of about 25 million (as against Sweden's 1 million) and could put huge, well-armed forces into the field. In July 1711, on the banks of the

Speak like a historian

Robert Massie, educated at Yale and at Oxford, is a journalist-turned-historian. An independent scholar, not attached to a university, he has published a number of popular prize-winning works on the Romanovs. His work on Nicholas II and his wife, *Nicholas and Alexandra*, was the basis for a successful film of the same title. Though his work is highly readable and informative, he is more likely to take up a definite position than to point to 'ifs and buts'.

Compare this passage with those in Question 6 at the end of the chapter.

The war of 1711, which led to the campaign on the Pruth, was not of Peter's asking; it was Charles who had instigated this fight between Russia and the Ottoman Empire. Nevertheless, once war came, Peter, still flushed with his success at Poltava, accepted the challenge with confidence and took rapid steps to prepare. Ten regiments of Russian dragoons were dispatched from Poland to watch the Ottoman frontier. Sheremetev with twenty-two regiments of infantry was ordered to march from the Baltic to Ukraine. A new, exceptionally heavy tax was levied to support the coming military operations.

Source: Robert K. Massie, *Peter the Great: His Life and Work* (Head of Zeus: Kindle edition; 2012), 568.[5]

Key terms

Janissaries: elite Turkish troops, technically slaves of the Sultan recruited from Christian subjects and converted to Islam. Like Guards regiments in 18th-century Russia, they could sometimes overthrow a Sultan or determine the succession through a palace coup.

Grand Vizier: the Ottoman Sultan's chief minister.

River Pruth, 38 000 Russians found themselves trapped by 130 000 Tartars and Turks. Peter's errors and situation were not unlike those of Charles XII in 1709.

The first Turkish assault was so shredded by Russian artillery fire that the **janissaries** urged the Turkish **Grand Vizier** to open negotiations. Peter, on the other hand, not knowing how much the Turks had suffered, did not counterattack but withdrew to a fortified camp. A Turkish assault on these new defences failed, at a loss of 8000 men, to 3000 Russian casualties, but the Russians were now encircled and short of supplies and ammunition. Disaster was averted only when, on 12 July, the Turks offered unexpectedly moderate peace terms.

Azov and its surrounding territory was to be handed over to the Turks and the fleet there was to be burnt. Taganrog would be razed to the ground. Peter also undertook to stay out of internal Polish affairs, allow merchants free passage and permit Charles to go home unmolested. Peter, who had expected to have to surrender all his Swedish conquests except St Petersburg, was mightily relieved.

Why did the Turks let the Russians off so lightly? The Russian defences had already proved hard to breach and there was serious discontent in the Turkish army. A Russian detachment had already destroyed the Turks' major gunpowder store at Braila on the Danube, so the Turks, too, were short of ammunition. Finally, the Grand Vizier had nothing to gain by restoring Charles XII's lost northern provinces. Charles had become an embarrassment to the Turks and a Swedish alliance made no sense to a government anxious to be at peace with Russia.

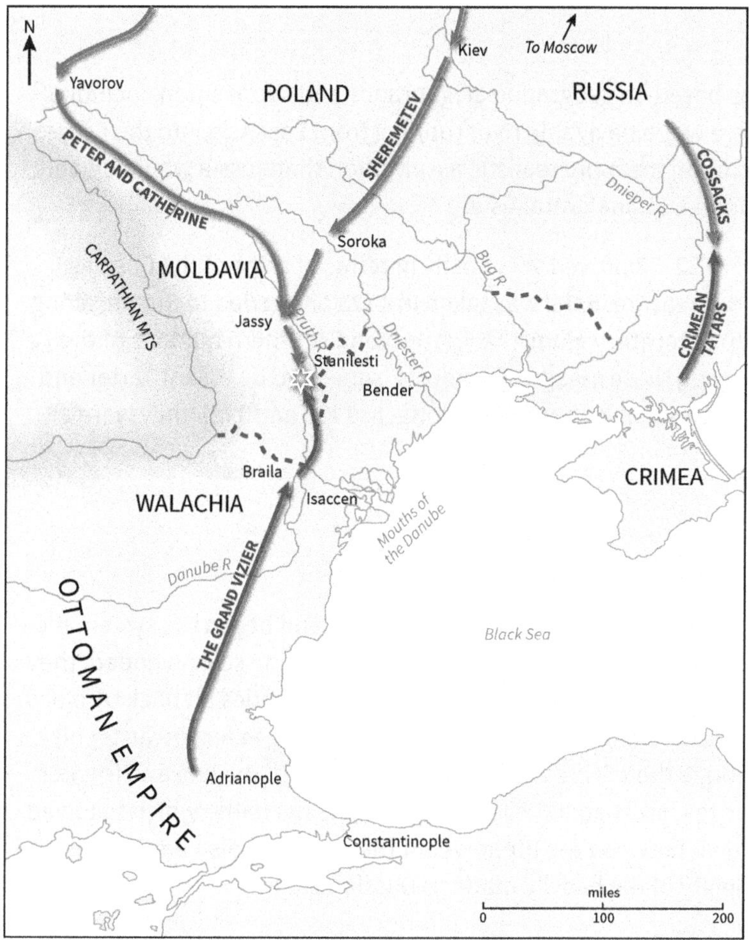

Figure 2.8: The Pruth campaign

The Treaty of Adrianople, 1713

Peter did his best to avoid carrying out all the terms of the Pruth agreement, especially the evacuation of Azov. However, the Turks now had the upper hand and in 1713 he was forced to end the war by a formal treaty signed at Adrianople. This agreement repeated the terms of the Pruth accord with the addition that, in order to keep what remained of their southern territories, the Russians must pay tribute to the Crimean khan.

War with Persia

By 1721, with peace with Sweden assured, the time seemed right to resume Russian expansion in the south – again suggesting that the south rather than the north was the preferred axis of expansion. Victory over Persia, Peter thought, would bring at least three great benefits – one defensive, one religious, the third breathtakingly expansionist:

- greater security against the still-formidable Turks;
- support for persecuted Christians;

ACTIVITY 2.8

Construct an answer to the following essay question:

'Why were Peter's campaigns against the Turks and Tartars so unsuccessful?'

- access to India and beyond – perhaps even to the extent of rerouting European trade with Asia, which normally took the seaborne journey by way of the Cape of Good Hope.

The third goal was based on geographical ignorance and supposition, including the belief that there was a navigable river running from East Asia into the Caspian Sea. It also rested upon the more realistic assumption that Russia would be able to exploit political upheavals in Central Asia.

The campaigns of 1722–23 proved very costly in terms of ships of the Caspian squadron, men and treasure. Baku was taken in 1723 and ceded to Russia, along with a narrow strip of territory along the western and southern margins of the Caspian Sea. However, these meagre conquests, subject to incessant Tartar and Turkish raids, were impossible to retain for long. In 1733 and 1735 they were all given up.

War with Sweden again

The Battle of Cape Hango, July 1714

In April 1713 Russian forces invaded southern Finland and began the systematic conquest of the province. By October when the campaigning season ended, they had made substantial gains. In the summer of 1714 the Swedes hit back by placing their fleet across the invading force's supply routes, forcing Peter to muster his Baltic fleet to dislodge them. However, the Russian ships of the line and frigates were not ready for sea, and had to be left behind. Thus the battle which followed became a showdown between the firepower of the great Swedish battleships and frigates and the agility of the heavily manned Russian galleys.

The Russian relief force feinted seawards in a calm, forcing the Swedes to counter by using small boats to tow their unwieldy ships further off shore. Once there the Swedes could not easily return. The Russian galleys, oar-powered and so largely independent of the wind, pushed through the gap and came to grips with a much smaller Swedish detachment off Cape Hango.

The Swedish commander had only one three-masted ship, the *Elephanten* of 14 guns, six galleys and three small skerry boats against over 90 Russian galleys crammed with men. The Swedish commander made the most of his firepower by aligning his ships between two islands, forcing the Russians to attack him head-on. Twice the Russians were thrown back but on the third attempt, led by Peter himself, they closed with the Swedes in hand-to-hand combat. At last the superior Russian crew numbers began to tell. One by one the Swedish vessels were taken until, at the end of three hours of fierce fighting, the *Elephanten* was overwhelmed.

The battle did not destroy the still-powerful Swedish fleet but it was decisive in allowing the Russians to break through the Swedish blockade, relieve the Russian forces in southern Finland and enable completion of the conquest. In the autumn of 1714 the Russians staged the first of numerous landings in Sweden itself. At the same time, with the Swedish Empire clearly falling apart, Peter found allies anxious to win a share of the spoils: Prussia in 1714 and Hanover the following year. However, neither Prussia nor Hanover was a reliable friend, and other states, notably Denmark and Britain, were alarmed at the dramatic rise in Russian power.

They were particularly worried by a Russian alliance with the ruler of Mecklenburg, a state in north-west Germany. British and Dutch suspicions even prevented an understanding with France when Peter visited that country in 1717.

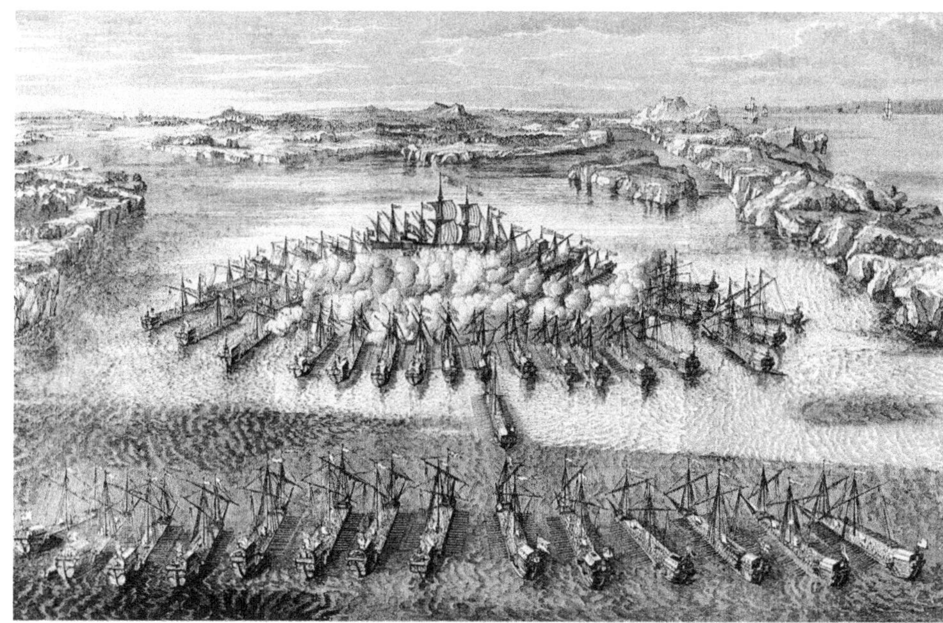

Figure 2.9: The Battle of Hango by the French engraver Maurice Baquoy

The peace congresses, 1718–1720

With Russia thus lacking friends and allies, the way was open for serious peace talks. The conference opened at Lövo in the Aaland Islands in May 1718 and a workable deal was quickly agreed. Sweden would give up the Baltic provinces in return for the aid of 20 000 Russian troops against Hanover and permission to take Norwegian territory from Denmark. It was wrecked on 11 December by the death of Charles XII while besieging Frederickstein in Norway. Under Charles's daughter, his unpopular foreign minister was executed and the war dragged on. In 1720 Peter responded with a large-scale landing in Sweden and promised British naval support for the Swedes failed to materialise. The new king, Frederick I, had no option but to sue for peace.

The Treaty of Nystadt, 1721

Russia made sweeping gains along the Baltic coast, including Livonia, Estonia, part of Karelia, and Finland. Free trade was agreed between the two powers and Sweden received a large cash payment for giving up Finland. Russia was now a great power on the fringes of Europe, a more frightening threat to the other European states than the Turks. Even in London ministers worried about the new Russian navy's potential to dominate the Baltic and hence Britain's vital source of naval stores. If Peter had built on foundations laid by others, the final structure of Russian might was his own achievement.

Timeline

1707–08	Don Cossack revolt under Bulavin
1708	First local government reform
1708	Bashkir revolt
1709	Battle of Poltava
1711	Senate created; *fiskals* introduced
1711	Battle of the Pruth
1712	Peter's marriage to Catherine, his second wife
1713	Treaty of Adrianople
1714	Inheritance law
1714	Battle of Cape Hango
1715	Second local government reform
1716	Military Regulation
1718–20	Administrative Colleges introduced
1721	Treaty of Nystadt
1721	Most Holy Directing Synod
1722	The Table of Ranks
1722–23	Persian War
1724	Soul tax introduced
1725	Death of Peter.

Further reading

All the books mentioned at the end of Chapter 1 are relevant here. You will find the level of detail in Massie's *Peter the Great* (Head of Zeus: Kindle edition, 2012) particularly useful. If you want to go from there to discover more about the historiography, the discussions in Lindsey Hughes's book should be very helpful. It's a big volume so use the index selectively to focus upon topics that particularly interest you.

Practice essay questions

1. To what extent was the Russian economy transformed between 1707 and 1725?
2. 'The years 1707 to 1725 saw almost no change in Russian society.' How far do you agree with this judgement?
3. How far were Peter's reforms in the years 1707 to 1725 driven by the demands of his foreign policy and wars?
4. How successful was Peter I in expanding the boundaries of Russia?
5. With reference to extract A and B and your understanding of the historical context, how do these explanations of the purposes of the 'Drunken Synod' differ? Which argument do you find the more convincing, and why?
6. With reference to extract C and D and your understanding of the historical context, which of these two extracts provides the more convincing interpretation in relation to the outbreak of war with the Ottoman Empire?

Extract A

The Drunken Synod, created when Peter was eighteen, continued its tipsy existence until the end of the Tsar's reign, with the mature man who had become an emperor continuing to engage in the same coarse buffoonery begun by an unbridled adolescent . . . In fact, it was partially in order to provoke, dismay and degrade the hierarchy of the church, and especially the new Patriarch Adrian, that Peter had originally instituted the Drunken Synod. His mother and the conservative boyars had had their victory over his own candidate, the more enlightened Marcellus of Pskov – so be it! – but Peter retaliated by appointing his own Mock-Patriarch. The parody of the Church hierarchy not only gave vent to his own resentment, but, as the years went by, reflected his continuing impatience with the whole institution of the Church in Russia. . . In Peter's own eyes, the buffoonery of the Mock-Synod was not blasphemous. Certainly, God was too majestic a being to be offended by his little parodies and games. Ultimately, that was what the revels of the Mock-Synod were: games. They were a form of relaxation – clownish perhaps, ridiculous, even gross – but for the most part, the Company were not men of refined sensibilities.

Source: Robert K. Massie, *Peter the Great: His Life and Work* (Head of Zeus: Kindle edition, 2012), 127.

Extract B

The purpose of these childishly provocative ceremonies remains obscure. There is no doubt that Peter himself attached importance to the 'Synod': he wrote out its relatively complex rules with his own hand and revised them several times. A generation later one of the last acts of his life was to attend one of its meetings. Certainly, therefore, it was not the casual outcome of youthful high spirits. Nor is it likely, as used to be thought, that it resulted from the tsar's failure in 1690 to secure the appointment as patriarch of the candidate he himself favoured. It has sometimes been argued that the 'Synod' reflects nothing more serious than the tsar's odd taste in amusements and his dislike of the deeply felt conventional piety of his subjects. But it may also have embodied a half-conscious attempt, by satirizing the formal and conventional aspects of religion, to devalue them and to assert that it was by daily conduct, not ritual observances, that the sincerity and value of belief must be measured. More probably, however, the brutal grossness of its activities reflects a dark side to Peter's character which is difficult for the historian to explore, pathological distortions of feeling whose nature he himself did not really understand.

Source: M.S. Anderson, *Peter the Great* (London: Pearson Education, 1995), 121–122.

Extract C

At first Peter did all he could to limit the effects of this unwelcome complication. In January 1711 he tried, in a letter to the sultan, to avoid the outbreak of full-scale war, while approaches were made both to the powers of the Grand Alliance and to France for possible mediation. When, however, it became clear by the spring that a war with Turkey would have to be fought (the Russian declaration of war, a response to the Turkish one several months earlier, was issued only on 11 March) he began to form far-reaching plans. For a decade or more it had been clear that in such a war Russia might hope for some active support from the Orthodox Christian population of the Balkans . . . Now in the spring of 1711 a Russian ruler attempted for the first time to play this potentially powerful religious card in a struggle with the Ottoman empire. In March a 'Proclamation to the Montenegrin People' and a 'Proclamation to the Christian Peoples under Turkish Rule' were issued. Both were explicit calls to revolt; and they were followed by a series of other appeals of the same kind.

Source: M.S. Anderson, *Peter the Great* (London: Pearson Education, 1995), 70–71.

Extract D

There is reason to believe that Peter was not averse to the prospect of a 'short, victorious war' in the south. The switch of attention to the Baltic in 1700 had been caused by international circumstances (notably the collapse of the Holy League . . .) as much as by any overwhelming preference for pursuing conquests in the north. Peter was almost as pleased with Azov as with St. Petersburg . . . he even diverted workers initially intended for St. Petersburg to work there. A new Turkish war offered opportunities for propaganda to Russians still basking in the glory of Poltava and the Baltic campaign. A Russian victory would change the political map of south-east Europe and speed up a solution in the north by depriving Sweden of a potential ally. There was also the religious factor. The 'Third Rome' doctrine had its strongest practical appeal not in the sixteenth century . . . but in the eighteenth, when it became possible to act upon it. If we take into account the more ambitious hopes, dormant until now, of further expansion into Ottoman lands and a crusade against the infidels, then it is easy to see that although Peter may have regretted the timing of the Turkish declaration of war, he had good reason for reviving his southern policy.

Source: Lindsey Hughes, *Russia in the Age of Peter the Great* (New Haven and London: Yale University Press, 1998), 46.

Taking it further

'Peter I was far less interested in a window on the Baltic than with acquiring an outlet to the Black Sea.' How valid is this interpretation?

Chapter summary

After studying this chapter, you should be able to make informed judgements about:

- the success or otherwise of Peter I's foreign policy and wars in the same period
- change and continuity within the Russian economy
- Russian society's exposure to the West
- reforms in government
- the nature, degree and gravity of opposition to Peter
- the changing role of the Orthodox Church
- Russia's emergence as a Great Power
- the degree to which autocracy was strengthened between 1707 and 1725.

End notes

1 Blanc S. 'À propos de la politique économique de Pierre le Grand', *Cahiers du monde russe et soviétique*, vol. 3, no. 1 (1962), 127.

2 Falkus ME. *The industrialisation of Russia, 1700–1914.* London: Macmillan; 1972, 22.

3 Anderson MS. *Peter the Great.* London: Pearson Education; 1995, 111.

4 Anderson MS. *Peter the Great.* London: Pearson Education; 1995, 120.

5 Massie R. *Peter the Great: His Life and Work.* Head of Zeus: Kindle edition; 2012.

6 Anderson MS. *Peter the Great.* London: Pearson Education; 1995, 128.

7 Anderson MS. *Peter the Great.* London: Pearson Education; 1995, 172.

8 Cited in L. Hughes *Russia in the Age of Peter the Great.* New Haven and London: Yale University Press, 1998, 3.

PART 2: ENLIGHTENMENT RUSSIA, 1725–1796

3 The epoch of palace coups, 1725–1762

In this chapter we will consider the degree to which Peter's reforms endured during the period of turbulence and political instability between his death and the accession of Catherine the Great. We will look into:

- The legacy of Peter the Great: the Service State; the role of the Church; the nobility, gentry and serfdom; Russia's involvement in international affairs.
- Disputed successions: and the role of the Supreme State Council and the Preobrazhensky Regiment.
- Tsarina Elizabeth: accession to the throne; education and Westernisation; legal reforms; taxation.
- Social developments: the redefinition of the Service State; serfdom and serf unrest.
- Foreign affairs: intervention in Poland; failure to secure the Crimea; involvement in the Seven Years War.
- Russia by 1762: the extent to which Petrine reforms survived; the accession of Catherine the Great.

The legacy of Peter the Great

Peter had brought dramatic reforms to Russia, but at the cost of noble resentment and widespread peasant resistance. In many ways these reforms were superficial. Obliged to concentrate his resources upon the armed forces, he had been unable to develop a modern education system that gave adequate training to his servants. His secular cipher schools never prospered and, within a few years of his demise, much schooling was back in the hands of the Orthodox Church.

Thanks to Peter the empire was now self-sufficient in timber, iron and copper, textiles were thriving, and the value of Russian exports was double that of imports. However, the rural economy was still the overwhelmingly dominant factor and, despite the expansion driven by Peter's soul tax, it was in a parlous state. Food prices, driven by internal customs duties and by the vast Russian distances, were high: a pood of grain from Kursk cost 1600 times its original value by the time it reached St Petersburg. Farm methods remained primitive and credit facilities, which might have produced landlord-led improvements, were primitive and interest rates high.

The Service State

Through the Table of Ranks Peter had attempted to codify the Muscovite tradition of a service nobility. By the end of the reign he had created a bureaucracy which would confer some degree of stability upon the regimes of his six indifferent successors. Although even after his death nobles itched for release from the constraints Peter had forced upon them, imperial service continued to be an attractive, prestigious and even economically essential career path. It also tended, for good or ill, to weaken local and regional loyalties in favour of the centre. One might tentatively agree with Geoffrey Treasure that 'The state was coming to be more important than its most privileged subjects'.[1] However, the lack of competent trained personnel made for inefficiency and **peculation**, and it was difficult to recruit anyone at all for the backwaters of local government. In the regions the Service State, where it worked at all, was threadbare, inefficient and corrupt.

Key terms

Peculation: embezzlement, or stealing of money entrusted to one's care.

Expropriate: to seize the property of a private individual or institution.

Dvoriane: Russian landlord class, comprising the titled nobility and the untitled gentry.

The role of the Church

Under Peter I the Orthodox Church had been reduced to the role of a department of state. Although its property had not been **expropriated**, its revenues were easily turned to secular state purposes. Peter had broken its educational monopoly. However, as we have seen, the Church had disliked his reforms and his apparent affinity for foreigners, leading to serious doubts as to his own orthodoxy, something which strengthened the opposition to his rule. (A little later in the 18th century, Peter III's apparent sympathy for Lutheranism also contributed to his overthrow.)

The nobility, gentry and serfdom

The titled nobility and the untitled gentry together made up the landlord class, the ***dvoriane***. Whereas the ancient titled nobility were often very wealthy and active in top politics, the mass of landholders were extremely poor. We have seen that the expansion of serfdom to public works and industry was a necessary consequence

Key terms

The Porte: the name of the court of the Ottoman Sultan at Constantinople. It is often used as shorthand for the Turkish government that met there, rather as 'Versailles' is used in relation to France in this period or 'Downing Street' in today's UK.

'Hat' party: a Swedish political group, named after their three-corned hats, that was active from 1719–1772 and ruled Sweden between 1738–1765.

Primogeniture: inheritance by the eldest son or, failing that, the closest male relative, all sons taking precedence over daughters.

ACTIVITY 3.1

Prepare for and conduct a class debate on the proposition 'Peter I had established a stable and modern autocracy in Russia'. You should take account of a range of different areas of Russian life.

Figure 3.1: Catherine I by Jean-Marc Nattier, 1717

of the rapid changes brought about by Peter. Because local government was so weak and rudimentary, millions of serfs had access only to the justice provided by their landlords' courts and flight was a major problem. Yet the *dvoriane* aimed at still greater authority over their serfs, just as they aimed to loosen the state's demands on themselves.

Russia's involvement in international affairs

Peter had made the Russian army, fed by a population expanding more rapidly than anywhere else in Europe, into a formidable force. Russia was now the major power in Eastern Europe, overshadowing even the Habsburg Monarchy and providing a serious challenge to the Ottomans in the south. Sweden, the major Baltic power, had been decisively defeated, though far from eliminated; Poland was almost a client state; and Russia was now a considerable naval power. However, none of this achievement was secure. French influence competed with Russian in Sweden, Poland and at **the Porte**, and in Sweden the mercantilist **'Hat'** political party longed for revenge.

Disputed successions

As we have already seen, there was no clear law of succession in Muscovy, a circumstance that engendered frequent palace revolutions. There was nothing resembling the **primogeniture** common in the West, and certainly nothing to prevent the accession of a female, or to prevent a claim through a female relative. In France, by contrast, a king had to be the nearest legitimate relative in the male line, a rule which almost always narrowed the field to one candidate. In this respect Russia was more like the Ottoman Empire, where the death of a Sultan began a scramble among numerous sons of numerous wives.

Peter I attempted to rectify this by crushing the Streltsy, dealing ruthlessly with his own son Alexis and affirming the Tsar's right to name his or her own successor. That did nothing to appease those who felt they ought to have been chosen, or to prevent them taking action once the sovereign was dead. And the plotter of midnight coups had a new weapon to hand, the Guards regiments, more coherent and effective than the Streltsy, and packed with young noblemen on their way to high rank and office. Only a ruler's failure to name a successor could have made this situation worse.

The succession and the role of the Supreme Privy Council

Catherine I, 1725–1727

Peter himself died before nominating his heir, an omission which immediately threatened to undermine the stability of the absolute state he had built. Would he be replaced by:

- Catherine, his widow, who favoured the reformers?
- Peter, his grandson (Alexis's son), the candidate of the conservative nobles?

The Senate assumed, probably correctly, that he would have chosen his second wife, Catherine, over his grandson, Peter. After all, she had been his constant companion, even on campaign, and he had had her crowned empress. Moreover, she was popular with the Guards regiments, a fact skilfully exploited by Menshikov: when the Preobrazhensky Regiment declared for her, all opposition vanished. In 1726 Catherine created a new executive body, the **Supreme Privy Council**, to which Menshikov was, of course, appointed. He was joined by his five original fellow councillors, who included Andrei Ostermann, Peter Tolstoy and Gavrila Golovkin, the veteran president of the College of Foreign Affairs.

Key term

Supreme Privy Council: also known as the Supreme State Council. At first merely advisory, the Council took over direction of government from the Senate and the presidents of the Colleges. After Catherine's death it was expanded to eight members, six of whom were drawn from the Golytsin and Dolgoruky families, the other two positions being retained by Ostermann and Golovkin.

Peter II, 1727–1730

Figure 3.2: Tsar Peter II by G. Mochanov, around 1730

In the event, Catherine's reign was short. When she fell ill in 1727, Menshikov prepared the succession of Alexis's son, as Peter II. His former colleague Tolstoy, knowing that his role in bringing down Alexis had not been forgotten, tried to bring in Peter I's second daughter, Elizabeth. He failed, and Menshikov was briefly able to prolong and expand his power through his control of the new Tsar. But before

Figure 3.3: Empress Anna Ioannovna, (1693-1740), 1730.

Key terms

Conditions: the terms the Council attempted to impose upon Tsarina Anna in 1730, when she succeeded to the Russian throne.

Oligarchy: a system of government which concentrates all power in the hands of a small group of individuals. It is often perpetuated by retaining that power within a network of those few individuals' families.

ACTIVITY 3.2

This is a period of bewildering changes of government and it is important to have a clear framework in your mind before getting buried in the detail. Make a list of rulers between 1725 and 1762 with their dates. Under each ruler list her/his key ministers and the dates (where known) of any changes.

Draw a family tree chart to remind yourself of the relationships.

the summer was out the Dolgoruky family had overthrown Menshikov and sent him into exile.

Anna and the 'Conditions' of 1730

Peter II's reign was hardly longer than Catherine's, though he had time to remove the capital temporarily to Moscow, a gesture symbolic of the Dolgorukys' determination to roll back reform. When he died of smallpox in 1730 he was succeeded, not by Elizabeth, but by Anna, daughter of Peter I's former co-regent, his half-brother Ivan V, and widow of the Duke of Courland. The Supreme Privy Council, now dominated by the Golytsins and Dolgorukys, chose her in an all-night sitting on 18–19 January 1730. Anna had the reputation of being inactive, submissive and indifferent to Peter's reforms, an ideal selection for great nobles determined to perpetuate their own power. To be quite sure, they determined to impose upon her a set of **Conditions** which severely limited her powers over finances, foreign policy and patronage. She would not be able either to marry or to name an heir; nor, without the consent of the Council, would she be permitted to make war or peace, levy or spend taxes, appoint senior civil or military officers, or grant titles or lands of estates. A delegation was sent to Mitau, the capital of Courland, to obtain Anna's acceptance.

Who was behind the Conditions and would they, had they lasted, have transformed Russia into a constitutional monarchy? The Soviet historian S.M. Troitsky and the Russian historian Alexander Yanov have argued that Andrei Golytsin regarded them as the beginning of a constitution along Swedish or Polish lines. The British historian Paul Dukes is more cautious, pointing out that 'neither the Dolgorukys nor Golytsin went explicitly further on paper than the Conditions'.[2] There was no long-term plan and no underlying political theory. In his view, the Conditions were no more than a means of retaining power in the hands of a particular faction.

Anna and the coup of 1730

Unfortunately for the Council, its security was less than perfect. The existence of the Conditions leaked to other nobles at court. They in turn spread the news among the nobles and gentry who had assembled in Moscow for Peter II's wedding and now remained for his funeral. Most of these were horrified by the Conditions, perhaps because to them autocracy was far preferable to domination by a narrow **oligarchy**. An opposition mission was sent hotfoot to Mitau: arriving shortly after the Council's emissaries, its members urged Anna to reject the Conditions.

Confronted by these alternatives, and aware of her popularity with the Preobrazhensky Regiment, Anna and her advisers played a shrewd game. To gain time she accepted the Conditions and started for Moscow, but she had no intention of abiding by them. When she reached the suburbs of Moscow she visited the Guards, served them vodka with her own hands and signalled her rejection of the Conditions by proclaiming herself their Colonel. With them at her back she then entered her capital, publicly tore up the Conditions, had her opponents arrested and abolished the Supreme Privy Council.

Tsarina Elizabeth, 1741–1761

Figure 3.4: Elizabeth of Russia by the Danish artist Vigilius Eriksen, around 1758

ACTIVITY 3.3

Make notes towards an essay on whether the Preobrazhensky Regiment can be regarded as the key factor in all of the coups between 1725 and 1741. You should gather together all the reasons for thinking that the Preobrazhensky Regiment was the key factor. Then note down all the reasons for thinking that other factors were also important, or as important, or more important. Review your notes: what is your own opinion, based on this evidence?

Accession to the throne

Anna died in 1741, having named her four-month-old nephew Ivan as her successor the previous year, with her favourite, Ernst Johan von Biron (Bühren), ruling as regent. Within three weeks Biron was arrested and exiled in a midnight coup organised by Field Marshal Münnich, after which Münnich and Andrei Ostermann, the Foreign Minister, competed for power. Their rivalry, combined with failure to ensure that they had a wide base of support within the nobility and the Guards, was fatal. Elizabeth Romanov, daughter of Peter I and Catherine, had been quietly building support for some time and had even approached the Swedes for military support. Crucially, her parentage, pleasure-oriented lifestyle and frequent visits to the Guard regiments won over the young nobles of the Preobrazhensky Regiment. On the night of 25 November she marched with them to the Winter Palace, where they arrested the infant Ivan VI and his parents, and detained Münnich. Elizabeth crowned herself empress on 25 April.

She moved quickly to secure her regime, exiling Ostermann and Münnich, and restoring some of the powers of the Senate. Thereafter Elizabeth proved barely more interested than Anna in the tedious details of government. However she was quite prepared to legislate to ensure that she had first sight of all fine imported cloth: at her death she left no fewer than 15 000 dresses, not counting the additional 5000 destroyed by fire some years earlier. Paul Dukes is particularly scathing about her appointments of 'erstwhile playmates' to high offices: her illiterate Cossack lover, Alexis Razumovsky, was made a field marshal.[3] Dukes is, however, a little more generous to the brothers Peter and Alexander Shuvalov, who took over domestic affairs; to the Chancellor, Mikhail Vorontsov; and to the capable Foreign Minister, Alexis Bestuzhev-Ryumin.

To secure her regime Elizabeth made sure that Ivan VI was safely imprisoned and found a successor of her own. She chose her orphaned German nephew, Peter of Holstein-Gottorp, who was brought to St Petersburg, formally converted to Orthodoxy and proclaimed her heir in November 1742. In 1745 she married him to another German Lutheran, fourteen year-old Princess Sophie of Anhalt Zerbst, who, on conversion, was renamed Catherine, in honour of Elizabeth's mother. After an anxious period of waiting, Elizabeth was rewarded with the birth of Catherine's son Paul in September 1754. On the face of it the dynasty was now safe for at least two generations.

Education and Westernisation

Education

Education in Russia was inadequate for the purposes of the Service State, but to widen it would certainly open Russia to uncomfortable Western influences, which might even undermine the autocracy. Peter's successors were even less inclined

Voices from the past

Peter and Alexander Shuvalov

Sons of a prominent Russian officer and cousins of Elizabeth's lover Ivan Shuvalov, the brothers dominated internal affairs for most of the reign.

Along with a third brother, Voronstov, the three Shuvalovs formed the core of the powerful pro-French faction at court. While Elizabeth was alive they successfully courted the future Peter III, who in 1761 made them both field marshals. On Peter's overthrow by his wife, Catherine, however, they fell from office.

Peter Shuvalov (1710–1762) had begun his career in Elizabeth's service long before her accession. When she became empress he was rewarded with the court office of Chamberlain, became a senator and was made a count in 1746. Allowed very extensive powers in both civil and military affairs, he experimented with army organisation and with new types of artillery. However, his most important innovation was the introduction of internal free trade in 1753.

Alexander Shuvalov (1710–1771) headed the Secret Chancellery, the political police, a post very useful when it came to eliminating enemies such as Bestuzhev.

to risk opposition and social instability, and education suffered accordingly. By the early 1760s the 26 Church grammar schools had only 6000 students, most of them theological students and sons of clergy. Other sources of education were rigorously vocational.

However, vocational education was not what many nobles wanted. Simon Dixon points to a much wider interest in Western culture than just its technology. Even the prestigious St Petersburg Cadet Corps had only 600 boys enrolled by the end of Elizabeth's reign and all schools provided an unpleasant experience. 'Russia's élite', as Dixon observes, 'tended to remember their schooldays as a nasty, brutish period that they would rather had been shorter'.[4]

The limits of literacy

Most nobles were educated at home by foreign tutors or received only rudimentary schooling and as many as 20% may have been illiterate. For example, by 1760 only 84% of male nobles could both read and write – and many a man in this category may have been able to do no more than sign his own name. Literacy rates were far higher among sons of clergy and in the newly acquired Baltic provinces, but almost non-existent for the Russian peasantry. Only peasants ascribed to some industrial enterprises saw any economic (or any other) advantage in learning to read and write. Dixon concludes that the 18th century made almost no difference at all to Russian literacy rates, hovering at about 6% for males and 4% for females. By contrast, the end-of-century figures for France were 47% and 27%, for Britain 68% and 43%; and for Prussia an astonishing 80% and 50%.

Westernisation

Literate or not, the nobility increasingly assimilated and adopted the more outward forms of Western culture. Most now wore Western clothing, and the urbanised upper nobility became very fashion-conscious. As we saw in Chapter 2, fine wines partly displaced vodka, and sugar supplanted honey. Under the surface, however, there was plenty of resistance to alien forms of behaviour and thought, and elite culture overlapped with popular peasant culture. For example, noble and peasant alike preferred the spoken to the written word, educated people preferring recitals above reading poetry. And the classes enjoyed similar physical pursuits. As Dixon points out, 'one did not have to be a peasant to enjoy sliding down the massive ice-hills that dominated Russian fairgrounds at Shrovetide'.[5] Elderly female fortune-tellers catered to all classes. Twice a week, Elizabeth provided bear-baiting as a public entertainment.

Nevertheless there was a distinct movement at the very upper end of society towards a more refined Westernisation. Russian architects were commissioned to design buildings incorporating ideas from Western books. Foreign books in German and French, including many translated from English, were sold or rendered into Russian every year. For example, almost 3000 French titles appeared in St Petersburg and Moscow between 1730 and 1760. Italian opera, delivered by visiting composers, singers and musicians, was as well established and well supported as in any European capital.

Legal reforms

In the Russian tradition, legislation, its interpretation and implementation were all the province of the autocrat, leaving almost no room for independent courts or for a legal profession trained to argue on the basis of underlying principles. Even Peter I's Military Regulation of 1716 had banned lawyers from criminal trials so that their long-winded arguments would not 'burden' the judge.

Codification

Then there was the question of codification. The absolute right of the autocrat to legislate had produced laws which were often ambiguous and frequently conflicting. Russian record-keeping was so poor that very often the texts could not be found. Peter I had recognised the problem and had ordered a codification based on a Swedish model, but he died before the work was completed and it was subsequently ignored. Another attempt between 1727 and 1730 achieved nothing, and yet another begun in 1730 was wound up under Elizabeth in 1744. In 1754 Peter Shuvalov persuaded Elizabeth to make one more attempt at codification.

A Codification Commission was set up and eventually produced a comprehensive report. It made no attempt to place specific limits on the ruler's authority, although Ivan Shuvalov later produced a memorandum recommending that the Tsar's actions should be subject to the law. However it did envisage far greater privileges for the nobility. Had it been implemented, the report would have ended compulsory state service, closed the service to non-noble entrants, ended the confiscation of estates belonging to convicted criminals, and exempted nobles from corporal punishments. The proposals came to nothing because of Elizabeth's growing indolence, combined with the outbreak of the Seven Years War.

Punishments

Despite the lack of lawyers' arguments, court procedures were often over-long and punishments were grotesquely severe. While, unlike Peter I, Elizabeth refused to take part in torture, she was quite willing to watch from behind curtains. In 1744 she abolished the death penalty, a measure which Dixon attributes to 'the combined humanitarian influence of court preachers and French novels' rather than to deep conviction or profound thought.[6] Indeed, she was happy to substitute nostril-slitting and branding, which was also the punishment for attempted flight and for those sentenced to exile. In 1754 women sentenced to exile with hard labour were exempted from mutilation but only because they were thought less likely than men to escape.

Taxation

Elizabeth's Russia was at war with Sweden from 1741 to 1743, notionally allied to Austria until 1748, and at war alongside the Austrians again from 1756 to 1761. Even in peacetime the costs of maintaining Russia's new-found prestige were enormous. The court, embassies abroad and above all the armed forces demanded more and more spending. Where was the money to come from?

Improving revenues

Since Peter I's time the mainstay of Russian finances had been the 'soul' tax but, despite a growing population, its yield was almost static. A new census would have been time-consuming and desperately unpopular, while to raise the rate would only have encouraged peasant flight. In the long term, as Peter Shuvalov understood, the answer was to build a richer economy which in turn could yield more revenues. His 1754 abolition of internal customs duties and the creation of new state-financed credit facilities, through a Bank of the Nobility and the Copper Bank, were part of this wider economic reform.

ACTIVITY 3.4

Construct a table showing the extent of (a) change and (b) continuity under Elizabeth.

In the short term, new and increased taxes were needed. One way would have been to raise the rate of **obrok** levied on state peasants but that could have provoked serious serf unrest: it was not increased from 40 kopecks to 1 rouble until 1760. Instead Shuvalov turned to indirect taxes: internal excises on salt and alcohol, combined with price rises for both products. These levies turned out to be hugely unpopular but they did increase the state's income. Thus by the mid-1760s, while the poll tax's contribution fell to 30%, down from over 50% of state revenues under Peter I, the salt and alcohol monopolies yielded almost 35%. Even the burden of the Seven Years War produced more fiscal initiatives. Church revenues were diverted, and fees for merchants who collected the indirect duties rose markedly. To save money, the budgets for local government and public works were slashed.

Key term

Obrok: a form of poll tax paid by assigned serfs while away from their owner's property and thus unable to perform the usual labour services.

The problem of rising expenditure

However, not even Shuvalov's reforms could keep pace with military, court and bureaucratic expenditure. Russia, like other great powers, had to run a considerable deficit, which rose from around 8% in 1733 to 40–45% by 1762. Worse still, the auditing procedures introduced by Peter the Great were rudimentary at best and collapsed altogether in wartime. There was no central treasury: while even Peter had charged four different Colleges with revenue administration, by 1760 over 50 such agencies were involved. Perhaps the basic problem was a lack of currency: in many places payments were made in kind rather than in cash. Thus when in 1762 Peter III demanded a clear statement of his finances, none was forthcoming. In fiscal and economic terms the modernisation of Russia still had a long way to go.

Social developments

The redefinition of the Service State

Anna's reforms

As we have seen, Empress Anna paid far more attention to her personal pleasures and preferences than to the work of government. Nevertheless she was astute enough to reward her supporters by weakening the Service State.

- In 1730 she removed Peter's requirement that noble estates should pass to one heir.
- Compulsory naval service was abolished.
- In 1731 she created a Noble Cadet Corps, where sons of noble families could begin their military careers as officers instead of starting in the ranks.
- In the same year, nobles took over from the army the task of collecting their serfs' poll-tax payments.

- In 1736 she raised the age of entry to state service from 15 to 20 and lowered the length of service from life to 25 years. She also allowed families with two or more sons to keep one at home to manage the estate.

However, this emancipation was not as sweeping as it seems. The Cambridge historian Tim Blanning points out that even sons left on the family estates could be called up for the civil service if necessary. Moreover, implementing the 1736 measures was delayed by the outbreak of war with the Ottoman Empire and by an embarrassing torrent of applications to leave government service.

Elizabeth allowed, rather than encouraged, the further development of noble privileges. For example, the profitable business of distilling alcohol became a noble monopoly but did not remove the obligation to serve the state. The Codification Commission proposed sweeping changes but, as we have seen, came to nothing. Elizabeth was far more interested in trying on new dresses than in trying out new legal systems and, in any case, the Seven Years War intervened. Further emancipation had to wait until the brief reign of Peter III.

The Manifesto on the Freedom of the Nobility, February 1762

Peter III's Manifesto has been the subject of lively discussion between historians. Richard Pipes concluded that it ended compulsory state service and thereby created a noble leisured class never before seen in Russia. However, that view has been seriously challenged, especially by Paul Dukes and Simon Dixon who, like the famous 19th-century Russian historian Vasily Osipovich Klyuchevsky, see not the abolition of compulsory service, but only a contraction of its length.

In any case, many nobles continued to dominate the army and civil administration, a point made by British historian B.H. Sumner as long ago as 1944. State service was a socially proper occupation, and many nobles depended upon their salaries to make ends meet. This tendency was encouraged by the establishment in 1754 of the Noble Land Bank, which allowed nobles to mortgage their estates at 6% interest. Their consequent indebtedness made long-term state service all the more necessary, even to the outwardly wealthy. Over 90% of the Russian officers who fought in the Battle of Borodino in 1812 were nobles.

Key term

Barshchina: labour services, measured in days, owed by a servant to his lord. In certain regions and for state serfs, this was commuted into a money payment, *obrok*.

Serfdom and serf unrest

Between 1725 and 1762, as the nobles became more emancipated, so the condition of the serfs worsened. In 1730 serfs were forbidden to own any land of their own, and from 1732, their lords were allowed to buy and sell them like livestock. A serf could not leave his village, join the army or enter a monastery without permission, and lords could enforce severe, sometimes fatal, physical punishments. Peter II removed the serfs' right to be freed in return for military service, and in 1747 their landlords were permitted to sell them as recruits. Under Elizabeth, the practice of selling serfs without land became very common and in 1760 she allowed landlords to exile recalcitrant peasants to Siberia. The main purpose of the decree was to populate Siberia – all exiles became free on arrival – but the effect was to give landlords even greater power. Household serfs (domestic servants) were particularly vulnerable to abuse, and women most of all. All this was on top of the already heavy burdens of **barshchina**, *obrok* and taxation.

Sumner pointed out that, in theory at least, the 1762 edict removed the legal justification for serfdom. If nobles were allowed serfs in return for compulsory state service, how could serfdom be justified once state service ceased to be compulsory? Had Peter issued another manifesto freeing the serfs, only for it to be suppressed by the nobility? Sumner argued that this perception became very common among the peasantry, and probably contributed to the 1775 revolt of Emilian Pugachev (to which we turn in Chapter 4), who posed as the serfs' benefactor.

That analysis, however, fails to explain why there was no major peasant upheaval in Russia after Kondraty Bulavin (see Chapter 2) and before Pugachev. Nor does it help us to understand what other forms of resistance were employed and to what extent. As the historian David Moon has pointed out, 'The main conclusion to be drawn from the enormous efforts Soviet historians made to find evidence of a "peasant movement" in servile Russia is not how much peasant resistance there was to serfdom, but how little.'[7]

The limits of resistance

Simon Dixon argues that opportunities for successful organised revolt were few and slender. Behind the authority of the landlord lurked the military and legal power of the state, and the chances were further limited by conflicts among the peasants themselves. The very fact that peasant life centred around the *mir* (commune) and the individual household, both institutions demanding a high level of cooperation, produced plentiful occasions for dispute. Quarrels about who should be conscripted, or how land should be allocated, were frequent and often nasty. Extended peasant households, while essential as economic units, prevented most adult males from forming their own establishments before reaching their forties or fifties. This produced bitter internal rivalries, both between generations, and between adult siblings. And while such antipathies operated within communities, deeply rooted hostility to outsiders, the Tsar himself excepted, was even stronger. Collaboration between villages, let alone across regions, was rare.

Finally, and surprisingly, there were actually advantages to serfdom. In the south the army provided protection against Tartar raids, protection not available to refugee communities. More widely, it protected the serf from market forces such as devastatingly low prices for his produce and unemployment. No Russian serf took lightly to open rebellion.

Types of resistance

Nevertheless, peasants were far from passive. Banditry was still common along the highways and waterways. Until the mid-18th century, villages and towns were subject to pillaging raids, and even cities such as Moscow were not immune. It would be an error to see these outlaws as Robin Hood-like fighters against social injustice: many were simply violent criminals and their leaders were sometimes their own landlords. Nevertheless, it was often a form of social protest, though far from a threat to the autocracy.

Most peasants were not bandits but less violent or less dangerous alternatives were common. Flight, especially from conscription or from industrial ascription, was still a significant factor. At a lower level still, simple obstruction was almost

ACTIVITY 3.5

Why, in the years 1725 to 1762, did widespread peasant resistance not produce major uprisings? Draw up a list of possible reasons and put them into what you think is the order of their importance. Write a paragraph indicating which you think is the most important reason, and what the evidence is for this opinion.

universal. Dixon observes that 'deliberate lying, cheating and backsliding were among the most effective forms of "everyday" peasant resistance'.[8] One might conclude that there was plenty of resistance to serfdom, though little that was likely to overthrow the institution.

Foreign affairs

By 1725 Russia had three separate, but closely interlocked, areas of interest in foreign affairs:

1. **Sweden:** the Swedes were always looking for an opportunity – which the country's close friendship with France might provide – to wage a war of revenge.

Figure 3.5: Europe in the mid-18th century

2. **Ottoman Empire:** to Russia's south there were still motives and opportunities for expansion: Azov and Taganrog were yet to be recovered, the Crimea was yet to be conquered and there was still no outlet to the Black Sea. All these ambitions could generate war with the Turks.
3. **Poland:** conflict with Sweden or the Turks was likely to mean foreign intervention in Poland. Because the Polish monarchy was elective, every succession was bound to be disputed, allowing Sweden, France and Russia to fish in troubled waters, and the Ottomans to take advantage of Russia's periodic distraction.

Indeed, the first major conflict of the period, the War of the Polish Succession (1733–1735) was fought partly over whether a Russian or a French candidate should become king of Poland. In the next, the War of the Austrian Succession (1740–1748), Russia was nominally an ally of the Habsburg Monarchy, against Prussia and France, but was distracted, first by the intrigues that brought Elizabeth to power, then by a war with Sweden (1741–1743) and finally, by Elizabeth's sentimental affection for all things French. Not until 1746–47 did alarming French successes prompt St Petersburg to provide troops to support the British, Dutch and Austrians in Germany and the Netherlands. However, the Russian armies moved slowly and, although one expedition joined the Austrians on the Rhine, the war ended before they could come fully into play. The Treaty of Aix-la-Chapelle (1748) was concluded without Russia's participation and did not bring her any rewards.

The Seven Years War (1756–1763) was a different matter altogether: with Austria and France now allies, Elizabeth sent Russian armies against Frederick II of Prussia, and only her death in 1762 saved him from destruction.

Intervention in Poland, 1733–1738

The succession question, 1733

On 1 February 1733 Augustus II of Poland and Saxony died. The two principal candidates for the crown were the late king's son Augustus and the ex-king

Voices from the past

Andrei Ostermann, 1686–1747

Born into a middle-class family in the German state of Westphalia, Ostermann entered Russian service as secretary to one of Peter's admirals before attracting the attention of the Tsar himself. His command of several languages made him invaluable in negotiating the Pruth peace settlement with the Turks in 1711 and at the Åaland Islands conferences. He concluded the Nystadt treaty with Sweden, became Vice-President of the Foreign Affairs College, negotiated a commercial treaty with Persia and advised Peter I regarding his subsequent reforms. Catherine I gave him sole charge of foreign relations, and on her death he became governor to the young Peter II. Under the Empress Anna, as Vice-Chancellor of All Russia, he directed Russia's intervention in the War of the Polish Succession and the subsequent conflict with the Turks, and extended his considerable influence to domestic affairs. He was also responsible for Russia's victory over Sweden in 1741.

The accession of Elizabeth in December 1741 doomed both Ostermann's career and his anti-French policies. Arrested and sentenced to be broken on the wheel and beheaded, he was saved by a last-minute reprieve and permanent exile to Berezov in Siberia. He died there in 1747.

Stanisław I Leszczyński, who had ruled under the protection of Charles XII of Sweden from 1704 to 1709. Stanisław, now father-in-law to Louis XV, could count on French financial and military support, as well as the sympathy of Polish nobles who wished to escape dependence upon Russia. In September a Polish assembly, swayed by French money, overwhelmingly elected him king. In October a breakaway faction backed by Russia and Austria declared for Augustus. France promptly declared war upon Austria and Saxony, and a Europe-wide conflict began.

The War of the Polish Succession, 1733–1735

Unfortunately for Stanisław, the French preferred to campaign against the Austrians on the Rhine and in the north of Italy, rather than send substantial forces to Poland. In both Western theatres the French were victorious, aided by British and Dutch neutrality, an alliance with Spain, and Russian preoccupation with Poland. However, this French strategy left Stanisław almost defenceless when a Russian expedition, led by the Irish-born veteran Peter Lacy, marched on Warsaw. Stanisław fled to Danzig (modern Gdansk) where he was besieged by a new commander, Field Marshal Münnich. When Danzig surrendered in June 1734, Stanisław retired to another Baltic fortress, Königsberg, and from there to France. Some of his supporters, calling themselves the Dzikowska Confederation, fought on but were no match for the tough and numerous Russians. By the early spring of 1735 the war in Poland had ended.

Meanwhile, a Russian army, marching to the assistance of the Austrians, had reached Heidelberg on the Rhine, an alarming development which prompted the French to make peace. The fighting ended and in 1736 Stanisław abdicated, although the Treaty of Vienna was not signed until 1738. Under its terms Augustus II's son was confirmed as King Augustus III of Poland, while Stanisław

Voices from the past

Burkhard Christoph von Münnich, 1683–1767

Born in the north-west German duchy of Oldenburg, Münnich entered the French army at 17 and later served the German states of Hesse-Darmstadt and Saxony. By 1721, when he was invited to Russia, he was a capable military engineer and a major general. He quickly impressed Peter the Great with his plans for the fortifications of Kronstadt, the island guarding the sea approaches to St Petersburg, and Vyborg in Finland. In 1723 Peter put him in charge of the stalled building of a by-pass canal around stormy Lake Lagoda, part of a waterway linking the Volga to St Petersburg. Under Anna he was responsible for important reforms in military organisation and officers' pay. Münnich led the siege of Danzig in 1734 and distinguished himself as a field commander in the Turkish war of 1736–1739.

He was also a significant political figure, important enough to be rewarded by successive rulers as soon as they had established themselves on the throne:

- Catherine I promoted him to General-in-Chief;
- Peter II appointed him governor of St Petersburg;
- Anna made him a field marshal and (in 1732) President of the War College.

During the brief reign of Ivan VI, Münnich planned the coup that brought down Biron, only to be disgraced and exiled by Elizabeth in 1741. Freed by Peter III, he helped Catherine II to plan the revolution that brought her to power in 1762. He served her as Director General of Baltic Ports until his death at Tartu, in modern Estonia, in October 1767.

I Leszczynski was to be Duke of Lorraine for life. The Habsburgs and Spanish received some compensation in Italy.

Failure to secure the Crimea, 1736–1739

Figure 3.6: The Russo-Turkish War, 1736–1739

As one war ended, another began. Anna's government was convinced that Russia could now easily overrun Azov, Taganrog and the Crimea, while persistent Crimean Tartar raids provided a plausible excuse. For their part, the Turks were both confident of victory and worried by Russian successes in Poland. Indeed, had it not been for a simultaneous conflict with Persia, they might have entered the War of the Polish Succession.

In 1736 Russia declared war and at first achieved striking success: Lacy recovered Azov, while Münnich forced his way through the Perekop isthmus into the Crimea. Disease and casualties obliged both generals to withdraw, but in 1737 the Russians took Ochakov, at the confluence of the Dnieper and Bug rivers, so cutting off the Crimea from landward Ottoman assistance. Moreover, Austria entered the war and won early victories. Although Lacy failed to break into the Crimea, it seemed that Russia would quickly achieve all her objectives.

It was not to be. The Turks proved more formidable than expected and the allies found cooperation difficult. In 1738 Lacy again failed to penetrate the Crimea; in the same year Ochakov was lost. Even a successful invasion of Moldavia in 1739 did not make up for huge Russian losses and Austria's decision to withdraw from the war. St Petersburg had to sue for peace.

The 1739 Treaty of Belgrade gave both Azov and Taganrog to Russia, but only on condition that Taganrog remained unfortified and the Azov defences were levelled. Trade carried from these ports was to travel only in Turkish ships. Moreover, the

Crimea and the Tartar raiders it harboured were still independent. Thus, while the war had shown that the Russian army was now markedly superior to the Austrian army, it left the southern frontier fluid and demonstrated that the Ottoman Empire was still a dangerous foe.

The War of the Austrian Succession, 1740–1748

The next major European conflict was triggered by the death of the Habsburg emperor Charles VI, leaving only his daughter, Maria Theresa, to succeed to all his hereditary possessions. Because there was some doubt as to whether a woman could legally rule in some of these provinces, Charles had been hawking around Europe a document called the Pragmatic Sanction, an agreement that Maria Theresa should inherit all the Habsburg territories intact. Russia signed in 1726, in return for recognition of Peter's conquests and a promise of support in case of war against the Turks. By 1740 all the major powers had signed, each in return for specific concessions.

However, as soon as Charles was dead the ambitious new King of Prussia, Frederick II, claimed and invaded the rich Austrian province of Silesia. France at once supported Prussia against her old enemy Austria, while Britain backed Maria Theresa. There followed a complex series of conflicts in which Frederick and his ally, France, fought to retain Silesia and dismember the Austrian Empire. Maria Theresa, on the other hand, struggled to recover Silesia and to keep her empire intact. Russia, already an ally of Austria and wary of France, could have made a significant contribution to the Queen of Hungary's cause.

Russian aid to Austria and the Peace of Aix-la-Chapelle, 1748

Elizabeth's Foreign Minister, Bestuzhev, was convinced that Russia's real enemy was France and that her security was threatened by French intrigues in Sweden, Poland and Constantinople. He therefore tried to build an alliance of Russia, Britain, Austria and Saxony against France and Prussia. However, despite its rivalry with France, along with other European powers, the Russian court had a persistent tendency to admire French political and military power, and also French culture. In particular, France's King Louis XIV was taken as a model of how an absolute monarch ought to behave. Accordingly, Bestuzhev had to work against efforts to exploit Elizabeth's own sentimental preference for France. In the words of Hugh Ragsdale, he spent most of the war 'combating the plethora of intrigues by a strong and well-financed French party' for Elizabeth's support.[9] Thus, although Bestuzhev won an Anglo-Russian treaty in 1742 and another with Austria at the end of 1743, in March of the same year he had to accept a Russo-Prussian defensive agreement. His own position was not secure until well into 1744. It was not until 1746–47, when stunning French successes in the Netherlands and Germany threatened the whole European balance of power, that Russia engaged and sent troops to help Maria Theresa. Even then the Russian columns moved so slowly across Poland that their allies had to make peace without them. The Peace of Aix-la-Chapelle (1748) allowed Frederick II to keep Silesia, but otherwise provided for a mutual restoration of conquests in Europe, America and India. Russia took no part in the peace talks and gained nothing from them.

War with Sweden, 1741–1743

To make quite sure that Russia would not intervene, the French induced Sweden, where the Hat Party was now in power, to attack Russia in the Baltic. From the French point of view the ensuing war, which tied Russia up from 1741 to 1743, preventing any attempt to help Austria directly until 1747, was a highly desirable development. From the Swedish perspective it was a dismal failure.

At first the Swedish forces tried to drive the Russians from Finland and to threaten St Petersburg, thereby (they hoped) triggering a coup which would bring Elizabeth to power. (Elizabeth had secretly promised to return the conquered Swedish provinces if this help was forthcoming.) However, the Swedish navy was held up by an outbreak of plague and, although Elizabeth did seize power in November 1741, she revoked her earlier promise and her new foreign minister, Bestuzhev, continued with the war. The Russian navy established an overwhelming superiority on the Finnish coast and huge Russian land forces stormed Helsingfors (Helsinki) before overrunning the whole of Finland.

The Treaty of Åbo (1743) transferred only a small amount of territory in southern Finland to Russia: small, but strategically significant because St Petersburg was only a short distance away across the border. In return the Swedes had to accept Adolf Frederick of Holstein-Gottorp, uncle to Elizabeth's own nominated successor, as heir to the Swedish throne. For some time to come Sweden was dominated from St Petersburg and the Russian Baltic fleet was Stockholm's principal protection against Danish attack.

Voices from the past

Alexis Bestuzhev-Ryumin, 1693–1768

Bestuzhev was born into an old noble family, the son of a career diplomat. Educated in Copenhagen and Berlin, he entered the service of Peter I who, keen to see him trained in diplomacy, sent him to the Utrecht Conference in 1713 and allowed him to enter the service of the Elector George of Hanover. When George became King George I of Great Britain in 1714, he took Bestuzhev to his new kingdom and sent him from there to Russia to announce his accession. Bestuzhev returned to Britain, where he remained until 1721. In this way he acquired formidable diplomatic skills, together with a conviction that Russia's best interests would be served by alliance with Britain, the established enemy of France.

From 1721 until 1739 he was Russian ambassador at Copenhagen, after which he returned home to become a member of the Supreme Privy Council and an ally of Biron. When Biron fell in 1740 he was driven from court only to be rescued by Elizabeth, who, in 1741, appointed him Vice-Chancellor with responsibility for foreign affairs.

Bestuzhev was convinced that Russian interests in Sweden, Poland and the Ottoman Empire ran directly counter to those of France and therefore saw France's rivals, Britain and the Habsburg Monarchy, as natural allies. He was also wary of the aggressive ambition of Frederick II of Prussia.

His policy of alliance with Britain was fatally undermined by the unexpected Anglo-Prussian alliance early in 1756, and he was unable to prevent Russia's subsequent combination with France and Austria against Frederick. His friendship with Field Marshal Stephen Apraxin, who retreated after winning the battle of Gross-Jägersdorf in 1757, brought Bestuzhev down. Deprived of office, he was exiled to his estates until Catherine II recalled him to court in 1762. He died in April 1768.

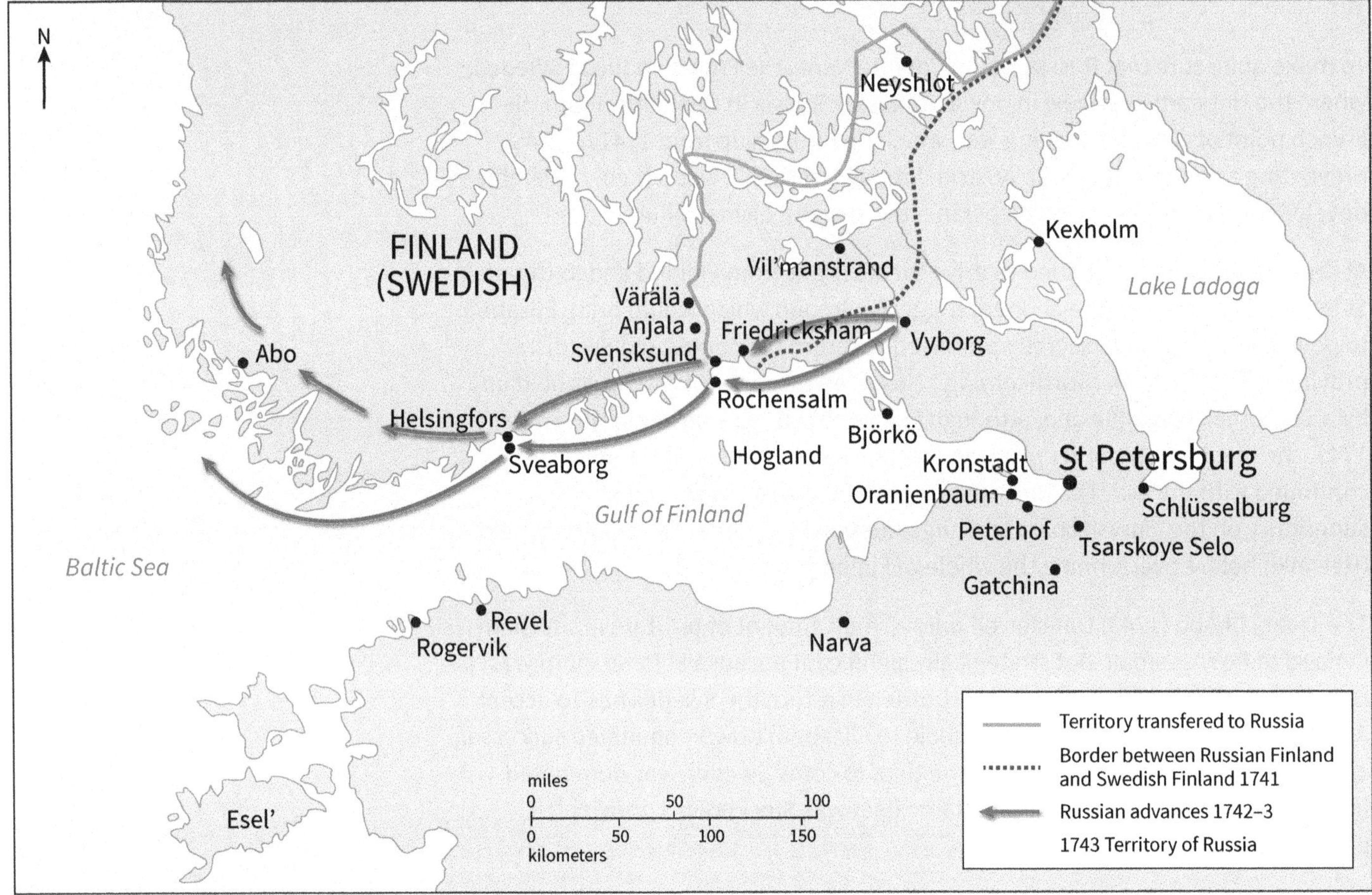

Figure 3.7: Russo-Swedish War 1741–1743

Involvement in the Seven Years War, 1756–1763

The Diplomatic Revolution, 1756

The War of the Austrian Succession had been indecisive and all the powers now reconsidered their alliances. Maria Theresa was very dissatisfied with Britain, which was principally a naval power and could not make a serious direct contribution to the recovery of Silesia. It made much more sense to join forces with Britain's main enemy, France, which was alarmed by the rise of Prussian power. Elizabeth, too, was now firmly anti-Prussian as well as pro-French, and in January 1756 Russia – Austria's ally and ruled by a pro-French empress – became part of this anti-Prussian coalition. Saxony also joined. Frederick II's only allies were Britain and Hanover.

Frederick struck first, invading and conquering Saxony in August 1756. He was immediately attacked by Austria and Russia, while the French conquest of Hanover laid him open to assault from the west. Frederick fought tenaciously, repelling the French with a striking victory at Rossbach and defeating the Austrians at Leuthen (1757). It was Russian intervention that turned the tide, transforming a potential Prussian triumph into a desperate fight for survival. Frederick could only hope that the pro-French Elizabeth, who suffered the first of a series of strokes as early as 1756, would soon be succeeded by the pro-Prussian Grand Duke Peter.

Figure 3.8: The Seven Years War

Gross-Jägersdorf and Zorndorf, 1757–1758

In 1757 a huge Russian force under Stephen Apraxin overran East Prussia and won the battle of Gross-Jägersdorf. Elizabeth and her court now expected him to overrun all of Prussia, but instead Apraxin withdrew across the Vistula to Russian soil. He was short of supplies and probably unwilling to invade Prussia when Elizabeth might suddenly give way to Peter. Elizabeth did not die: Apraxin was dismissed, his friend Bestuzhev was charged with treason and the new Russian commander, Villim Villimovich Fermor, resumed the invasion of East Prussia. When Frederick counterattacked, Fermor fought him to a bloody draw at Zorndorf (August 1758), a battle which taught Frederick II to respect the courage and tenacity of Russian troops. The next day Fermor was still on the field and within reach of a junction with the Austrians. But again Elizabeth's health and fears about the succession led the Russians to retire. Fermor was dismissed and the war went on.

Kunersdorf, 1759

In 1759 Fermor's successor, Nikolai Saltykov, at last joined hands with an Austrian corps and on 12 August met Frederick at Kunersdorf, near Frankfurt an der Oder. Frederick misread the terrain and badly underestimated his opponent. Saltykov anticipated Frederick's attempt to outflank him through dense forest, and the Prussians found themselves attacking the strongest part of the Russian positions. As evening drew on, Frederick launched a massive cavalry charge, only to see his horsemen bogged down in marshland and slaughtered by Cossacks and Kalmycks. Over half the Prussian troops engaged were killed, wounded or taken prisoner; the road to Berlin lay open; Frederick considered suicide.

For the time being Frederick was reprieved by allied differences over war aims and strategy, and by Austro-French fear of Russia. Saltykov fell ill and his replacement, Peter Rumiantsev, was well aware of the danger of regime change in St Petersburg. Nevertheless, by 1761 Frederick's enemies were slowly but surely closing in on him, limiting his room for manoeuvre and ensuring that his final defeat was only a matter of time. Rumiantsev took the great fortress of Kolberg, opening once again the road to Berlin. Worse, Britain withdrew the subsidies it had been paying to Frederick since the beginning of the war. Only Elizabeth's death on 5 January 1762 saved him from annihilation.

The Treaty of Hubertusburg and the Peace of Paris, 1763

The new Tsar, Peter III, at once withdrew from the war and turned his attention to a dynastic conflict with Denmark. However, there were, as Paul Dukes points out, deeper reasons at work than the new ruler's personal prejudices: 'Russia was beginning to realise that a Prussia defeated would not serve its interests any more than a Prussia triumphant, since a resurgent Poland or an expanded Austria could be at least as troublesome as a Prussia still intact but somewhat subdued.'[10] Now alone in her struggle, Maria Theresa was forced to accept the Treaty of Hubertusburg, whereby Prussia retained Silesia. At the same time (February 1763), the Peace of Paris gave Britain massive colonial gains at the expense of France and Spain. Russia, thanks to Peter's renunciation of all his country's conquests, gained nothing in terms of territory. But her military performance had won her the fear and respect of all the major powers. She was now unquestionably the dominant force in eastern Europe.

Russia by 1762

The extent to which the Petrine reforms survived

Military and diplomatic might

Peter I had made Russia into not only a major European power, but also the major force in Eastern Europe. Russia was represented by missions in all the major capitals and in many of the minor ones. The country's land forces expanded and became even more formidable in the years from 1725 to 1762, so much so that the Tsar was now feared in Paris and even in London. By 1756 Russia could field the largest army in Europe, its forces of all kinds totalling about 320 000 men. All this tended to overshadow the relative failure against the Turks and the Crimean Tartars.

As a naval power, however, Russia had gone backwards. The maritime service had never been popular among the nobility and Peter's successors had tended to ignore it. Paul Dukes makes the following telling comparison:

'Towards the end of the reign of Peter the Great, it will be recalled, the navy had consisted of 32 ships of the line, 16 frigates, 85 galleys and 20 or so sundry others, with a total complement of up to 28 000 men. By the early 1740s the numbers had declined to 20 ships of the line, 14 frigates, and 40 others of all kinds. The threat of war with Sweden and then with Prussia had meant some little increase in naval activity, but the overall size of the navy had not grown much and its quality had probably shrunk by the opening of the Seven Years War. While by 1757 there were 27 ships of the line, 14 frigates, 209 galleys and 11 others, almost half of them turned out to be incapable of managing more than the lightest of breezes, according to one assessment, while 11 of 27 transport ships sent to Kolberg sank on the way.'[11]

On the whole, however, Russia now counted for more in the European balance than any other land power.

The Service State

Peter I's attempt to permanently tie noble rank to compulsory service through his rigidly prescriptive Table of Ranks had clearly gone by the board by 1762. Nevertheless, as we have seen, neither Anna's changes nor Peter III's Manifesto totally removed it. It is indeed arguable that *de facto* economic need, ambition and social expectation were more effective forces than Peter's crude compulsion.

Social and economic change

Peter I strengthened the nobles' grip over their serfs and that grip was significantly tightened in the period up to 1762. Nobles received other privileges, such as the sole right to distil alcohol in return for four-year contracts to supply it to the state for a fixed price. Peter's policy of deliberately fostering a commercial middle class was far less important for his successors.

In terms of industrialisation, Peter had set Russia along the road to modernisation, and the fact that Russia was about to become the world's largest iron producer was a testament to continuing success. However, there had been no revolution in Russian agriculture, which was still based on serfdom and the three-field system of strip farming. The mid-century Russian economy thus embodied the main triumphs and the main weaknesses of the Petrine reforms.

The accession of Catherine the Great

Peter III's reputation

Why was Peter III successfully overthrown by his wife, the Grand Duchess Catherine? Accounts which rely on the later versions of Catherine's memoirs point to his alleged insanity, childishness (he loved to play with toy soldiers), utter incapacity (both political and sexual) and general unattractiveness as a husband. The problem here lies with the memoirs: Catherine produced at least six different versions, and her portrait of Peter (and of Elizabeth) becomes darker with each successive revision. In an early example she describes him as strikingly handsome and engaging.

In fact Peter III, in his eccentric, naive and youthful way, engaged energetically with the problems of government. As we have seen he immediately withdrew from the war, and then issued a manifesto calculated to secure the loyalty of the majority of the nobility, rather than just a narrow clique. He abolished the Secret Chancellery, made malicious denunciations more difficult and tried to tame those uniformed emperor-makers, the Preobrazhensky Regiment. For role models he chose two master-autocrats: Frederick II and Peter I. As the author Geoffrey Treasure puts it, 'He was more than a little odd, but certainly not the moron that his wife came to depict'.[12]

Speak like a historian

Historians often make a distinction between the situation as things are and the situation as they probably should be by law. *De facto* is a Latin expression meaning 'according to fact'. It contrasts with another Latin expression, *de jure*, which means 'according to law'. A rough equivalent would be to contrast 'in practice' with 'in theory'. If this use of Latin catches your interest, you might enjoy looking up, and perhaps learning to use, the following, which also frequently occur in history books: *ad hoc, terminus a quo, terminus ad quem, ante bellum, per annum, per capita, status quo, casus belli.*

Peter III's mistakes

Peter's downfall was that he offended too many vested interests without attracting sufficient counterbalancing support. The great court nobles may well have been alarmed at his attempt to attract wider support at their expense. In other ways he seemed to represent foreign interests. He abandoned the war against Prussia, calculating that disappointment at surrendering conquests would be balanced by relief at the onset of peace. If that was ever a realistic prospect, it was ruined by his attack on Denmark to recover the Duchy of Schleswig for his native Holstein. Much else that he did, profound or frivolous, made him look like a foreigner with foreign sympathies. He drilled his guards in a Prussian uniform. He announced that he would provide a Lutheran chapel for his German servants (immediately raising doubts as to the sincerity of his own conversion to Orthodoxy) and he introduced wider religious toleration. His confiscation of Church lands only reinforced this impression.

Crucially, he offended the Guards, whom he openly described as 'janissaries', without creating a counterbalancing force devoted to himself. The Preobrazhensky Regiment was humiliated by being relieved of its guard duties as punishment for what the British ambassador called 'idleness and licence'. Peter also tried to impose a severe Prussian-style discipline upon the whole army, and made nominal colonels drill their troops. As the prestige of the Guards sank, so the stock of Peter's Holstein regiment seemed to rise, exacerbating anti-German prejudices. Many of the ambitious young nobles in the guards' ranks feared that he would disband them altogether. They needed a saviour: should another claimant appear, he or she would have a willing military force close at hand.

Catherine and the coup

There were three possible candidates for the role of saviour: the still-imprisoned Ivan VI, Peter III's own infant son, Paul, and his clever and ambitious wife, the Grand Duchess Catherine. Catherine, now a focus for discontented nobles and courtiers, was by far the strongest of the three. She had probably made up her mind to seize power if she could, either through her son or in her own right, some years before. In June 1762 her current lover (one of a long line) was Gregory Orlov, a Guards officer with four influential and well-placed brothers. Other key allies were Paul's tutor, Nikita Panin, and Ekaterina Dashkova, sister to Peter's mistress.

It was Catherine who coordinated these disparate figures and planned the coup which she finally launched on 28 June 1762.

At dawn at St Petersburg she was proclaimed by three Guards regiments in succession, attended an impromptu church service and appeared with Paul on a balcony of the Winter Palace. Troops secured the city and its landward approaches and by early afternoon the forces on Kronstadt had been won over. Next morning her forces marched on the Tsar's residence outside the city, where Peter III was forced to abdicate. His estranged wife, now the Empress Catherine II, was just 33.

Figure 3.9: The coronation of Peter III, Catherine's eccentric husband. A portrait by Lucas Conrad Pfandzeldt, 1761.

Timeline

1725	Accession of Catherine I
1727	Accession of Peter II
1730	Death of Peter II; accession of Anna
1733–1735	War of the Polish Succession
1736–1739	Russo-Turkish War
1741	Death of Anna; reign of Ivan VI; accession of Elizabeth
1741–1743	Russo-Polish War
1756	Outbreak of the Seven Years War
1759	Battle of Kunersdorf
1761	Death of Elizabeth; accession of Peter III
1761	Russian withdrawal from the Seven Years War
1762	Manifesto on the Freedom of the Nobility
1762	Overthrow of Peter III; accession of Catherine II

Further reading

The most straightforward, yet thoughtful, account of the period is in Chapter 16 of Geoffrey Treasure's *The Making of Modern Europe 1648–1780* (London: Routledge, 2003). This can be supplemented by the clear but more challenging work of Paul Dukes in Chapter 4 and the first part of Chapter 5 of *The Making of Russian Absolutism 1613–1801* (London: Routledge, 1990). On Peter III, Catherine, her lovers and the coup, the first two chapters of John T. Alexander's gripping *Catherine the Great: Life and Legend* (Oxford: Oxford University Press, 1989) should be read critically but with great pleasure.

ACTIVITY 3.6

Plan and deliver a class presentation in answer to the question:

'Why was Peter III overthrown in 1762?'

Remember to:

- consider a wide range of factors
- develop and justify your causal hierarchy – your order of importance of the factors you have identified
- identify links between different causes
- consider different existing interpretations
- ensure that your argument runs throughout the essay.

Practice essay questions

1. To what extent had the Service State been dismantled by 1762?
2. 'There was no peasant resistance to serfdom between 1725 and 1762.' How valid is this statement?
3. How important was the Preobrazhensky Regiment in bringing about regime change between 1725 and 1762?
4. How far did Russia consolidate its position as a great power between 1725 and 1762?
5. With reference to these extracts and your understanding of the historical context, which of the three extracts provides the most convincing interpretation of the aims and effects of the 1762 Manifesto?

Extract A

[Anna's reforms] culminated in the Manifesto 'Concerning the Granting of Freedom and Liberty of the Entire Russian Dvorianstvo', issued in 1762 by Peter III, which 'for ever, for all future generations' exempted Russian dvoriane from state service in all its forms. The Manifesto further granted them the right to obtain passports for travel abroad, even if their purpose was to enrol in the service of foreign rulers – an unexpected restoration of the ancient boyar right of 'free departure' abolished by Ivan III. Under Catherine II, the Senate on at least three occasions confirmed this Manifesto.

Source: Richard Pipes, *Russia under the Old Regime* (London: Penguin, 1995), 133. (The first edition was published in 1974.)

Extract B

It should be recalled that, like the landed nobilities of other countries, the *dvoryantstvo* was far from a homogenous class. Some 80% of the serfs . . . were owned by 20% of the nobles. The 60% who had less than 20 'souls' and altogether owned but 5% of the total found state service essential if they were not to moulder in provincial poverty. The evidence suggests that it was attractive, too, to the better-off minority. That is why Peter's edict could be presented as generous recognition of a new spirit: 'We do not find that necessity for compulsion in service which was in effect up to this time'. Liberty was to be bestowed on the whole Russian nobility, not so that it could live in selfish sloth but to enable it to 'continue service both in Our Empire and in European states allied to us'. The emphasis throughout is upon continuance of service and on educating children to be fit for it. The decree has been seen as Peter's attempt to consolidate his rule on the basis of a gratefully loyal *dvoryanstvo*, an attempt to emancipate himself from the confining, jealous circle of magnates; that some of them moved so quickly to destroy him lends support to this view.

Source: Geoffrey Treasure, *The Making of Modern Europe, 1648–1780* (London: Routledge, 1985), 587–588.

Extract C

Although greeted with 'unimaginable joy', as one noble put it, and by a request from the Senate to commission a statue of the Tsar made of solid gold, the small print revealed a number of qualifications, not the least being that officers could not retire in wartime and civilian officials had to secure the permission of the Tsar. It was also firmly stated that those who did not volunteer for service would be excluded from court and denied imperial favour.

It used to be thought that this edict marked a watershed, not just in the history of Tsar–nobility relations, but also in the history of Russia in general. Richard Pipes, for example, was of the opinion that 'it is difficult to exaggerate the importance of the edict of 1762 … with this single act the monarchy created a large, privileged, westernised leisure class, such as Russia had never known before'. More recent assessments have been rather calmer, seeing the measure as partly a codification of existing practice and partly a recognition that compulsion was no longer needed to make nobles work for the state. If there was indeed a discernible move by some nobles from the army or administration towards the provinces, it did not alter the essentially autocratic nature of Tsarist authority or the essentially servile attitude of the nobility.

Tim Blanning, *The Pursuit of Glory: Europe 1648–1815* (London: Penguin, 2008), 243.

Taking it further

'The Russian state was less stable at the accession of Catherine II than at the death of Peter I.' To what extent do you accept this statement?

Chapter summary

After studying this chapter, you should now have a firm understanding of the reigns of the rulers that followed Peter the Great. You should understand why Russia became involved in a series of wars. You will have studied the economic and social situation in Russia, the changes attempted and the degree of change actually achieved. You should have a good level of insight into:

- the condition of Russia at the death of Peter I
- the reasons for the series of palace coups between 1725 and 1762
- the reasons for, and significance of, the series of wars between 1733 and 1763
- the degree to which the Service State had changed by 1762
- the degree to which the condition of the peasantry had altered by 1762
- the extent to which Russian society had been Westernised by 1762
- the extent and nature of Russia's position as a great power.

End notes

1 Treasure G. *The Making of Modern Europe, 1648–1780*. London: Methuen, 1985, 582.

2 Dukes P. *The Making of Russian Absolutism 1613–1801*. London: Longman; 1982, 105.

3 Dukes P. *The Making of Russian Absolutism 1613–1801*. London: Longman; 1982, 110.

4 Dixon S. *The Modernisation of Russia*. Cambridge: Cambridge University Press; 1999, 153.

5 Dixon S. *The Modernisation of Russia*. Cambridge: Cambridge University Press; 1999, 159.

6 Dixon S. *The Modernisation of Russia*. Cambridge: Cambridge University Press; 1999, 146.

7 Moon D. 'Reassessing Russian Serfdom', *East European History Quarterly*, vol. 26, no. 4 (1996), 495.

8 Dixon S. *The Modernisation of Russia*. Cambridge: Cambridge University Press; 1999, 106.

9 Ragsdale H. 'Russian Foreign Policy, 1725–1815', in D. Lieven (ed.), *The Cambridge History of Russia: Volume II: Imperial Russia, 1689–1917*. Cambridge: Cambridge University Press; 2006, 505–506.

10 Dukes P. *The Making of Russian Absolutism 1613–1801*. London: Longman; 1982, 125.

11 Dukes P. *The Making of Russian Absolutism 1613–1801*. London: Longman; 1982, 117.

12 Treasure G. *The Making of Modern Europe, 1648–1780*. London: Routledge, 1985, 587.

4 Catherine the Great and Russia, 1762–1796

In this chapter we will examine the changes brought about during the reign of Catherine II, often referred to as 'the Great'. We will be studying both internal reforms and external expansion. We will look into:

- Catherine: character and aims; extent of influence of the Enlightenment and the impact of the French Revolution on Catherine.
- Developments in central and local government: codification of the law; the Great Commission; reform of the Senate; changes to local government in towns and rural areas.
- Changes to society: the importance of landownership and the gentry; Enlightenment and education; reforms to religion.
- The economy and the persistence of serfdom and its impact on economic development.
- Opposition and rebellion: plots against Catherine and her reaction; the Pugachev Revolt and its consequences; Why did Pugachev fail?
- Foreign affairs and wars: Sweden; Turkey and Crimea; wars with Poland and its partition.

Catherine

Character and aims

Character

Catherine was an immensely ambitious, able, energetic and charismatic woman. Of her ambition there can be little doubt: she had had her eyes on the throne long before her husband actually became Tsar; she adroitly avoided becoming a mere regent for her son Paul; and she managed to keep Paul outside politics until her death in 1796.

Her energy was reflected in an active sex life: she never remarried but had at least 20 lovers. Paul may not even have been Peter III's son – despite a strong physical resemblance – in which case the last six Romanov Tsars were not Romanovs at all. Some of Catherine's men, notably Stanisłas Poniatowski, Gregory Orlov and Gregory Potemkin, were politically important; but she never allowed any of them to direct policy. That, of course, did not prevent the circulation of salacious myths, at the time and since. Frederick of Prussia's obscene remark to the effect that genitals drove Russian foreign policy was more witty than accurate – and there is no truth at all in the myth that Catherine died under the weight of a stallion!

Aims

There has been considerable debate about Catherine's use of the power she so ruthlessly acquired and kept. Was she simply interested in staying on the throne? Was her well-publicised attachment to the ideas of the Enlightenment genuine or merely a cover for a ruthless autocracy? Many historians now agree that she intended to use her authority for what she perceived as the public good. In her mind that included producing a centralised system of government, capable of assimilating all the varied faiths, ethnicities and cultures of her enormous empire. In terms of foreign policy she aimed to continue large-scale expansion at the expense of the Ottoman Empire, the maintenance of Russia's dominance in Poland, and security against the ambitions of Swedes, Prussians and Habsburgs. If she was only completely successful in attaining her first and primary goal – survival – her overall achievement was nevertheless formidable.

The extent of influence of the Enlightenment

What was the Enlightenment?

'The Enlightenment' is the name given to an intellectual movement of the 18th century which emphasised the improvement of the human condition through the application of reason. Drawing on the Scientific Revolution of the 17th century, 'Enlightened' thinkers argued that, if physical nature followed universally applicable laws such as Isaac Newton's laws of motion, surely there must be natural laws controlling government, laws, society and the economy – in short, every aspect of human life. If such laws could be discovered and applied, it would be possible to have an ideal system of governance, law and society. Such laws could be uncovered by the application of observation and reason.

Such natural laws were held to include equality, personal liberty, humane laws governing daily life and a contractual form of government – good governance

Speak like a historian

Catherine II's private life

Many male rulers, notably Louis XIV and Louis XV of France, were more sexually promiscuous than Catherine, yet their antics tended to be played down by contemporaries and historians, whereas Catherine's affairs still fascinate. This may be because the expectations placed on men were less rigorous than those for women. Consequently, Catherine and other prominent and powerful women who refused to conform became the targets of pornographic myth. Christina of Sweden, who never married, was reputed to have had a long-term lesbian affair; Louis XVI's Austrian wife, Marie Antoinette – a foreigner who ignored court etiquette – was (falsely) accused of innumerable affairs with both women and men. Catherine probably attracted such attention because she was at once a foreigner, a woman, a usurper and reputedly complicit in her husband's murder, as well as a sexual nonconformist.

in return for obedience. This did not necessarily mean government by a representative assembly. Indeed, it was arguable that some realms could only be governed by an absolute authority, and a benign absolute ruler should impose reforms from above.

The debate over 'Enlightened absolutism'

It used to be asserted that certain rulers did indeed consciously rule in accordance with the principles of the Enlightenment. The three main examples used by historians are Frederick II of Prussia, Joseph II of the Habsburg Monarchy and Catherine II of Russia, though others, notably Gustavus III of Sweden and Charles III of Spain, are sometimes included.

By the middle of the 1960s the whole concept of 'Enlightened absolutism' was becoming disreputable. It was attacked on the grounds that, although Frederick, Joseph and Catherine may have corresponded with men like Voltaire, and have given lip service to their reforming ideas, they were really driven by a desire for military power. Removing noble and clerical tax privileges produced greater income for the state and thus more soldiers. Economic reform, by increasing the country's taxable wealth, would have the same effect. Religious toleration brought skilled immigrants, and therefore a stronger economy and a larger pool of potential military manpower.

Rulers like Catherine were charged with hypocrisy and cynicism. Yet, in her way, Catherine was as ambitious a reformer as Joseph II of Austria. Unlike Joseph, she was able to spread her efforts over more than three decades as opposed to his one. She attempted only one goal at a time, and she knew when to accept defeat. In the end her patience and caution reaped greater fruits than his reckless eagerness.

The militarist interpretation of 'Enlightened absolutism' cannot explain reforms which had no obvious fiscal, policing or military benefit. Yet many rulers did

ACTIVITY 4.1

The leading thinkers of the Enlightenment were often French and were thus referred to by the French word '*philosophes*'. Conduct your own research into the ideas of some of them, especially Montesquieu, Diderot, Voltaire and Cesare Beccaria. Divide the names between members of the class and bring your results to a plenary session for discussion. On what points were the *philosophes* in agreement and on what did they differ?

Key terms

Liberalism: the principle of government through elected representatives of the people, the 'nation', with individual civil rights such as freedom of expression, association and assembly, and the security of private property. Liberals tended to want political rights for propertied men, not for the poor and landless or for women.

Nationalism: the idea that each nation should have its own state, a 'nation-state'; the attempt to defend the interests of a nation against supposed threats, typically from 'foreigners' at home or abroad.

Nation: conventionally a people with a common cultural, linguistic and ethnic identity. This is not the same as a 'nation-state'. Most states contain several languages, cultures and ethnicities. Many nations have not formed states but are part of one or more countries.

attempt such changes, such as providing orphanages, shelter for unmarried mothers and illegitimate children, hospitals, more humane prisons and legal systems, and assistance for the infirm. Joseph even forbade peasants to drink untreated water. Since the 1980s, therefore, scholars have argued that, although power was a primary objective, some rulers genuinely set out to improve their subjects' lives. As Tim Blanning points out, 'not even [Joseph II] could have hoped to transform a deaf and dumb blind crippled lunatic illegitimate unmarried mother into an effective fighting unit'.[1] Similarly, there is now broad agreement that a number of Catherine II's reforms cannot be explained away by military advantage. Thus the idea of 'Enlightened absolutism', though modified, is still alive and well.

How enlightened was Catherine?

The modern consensus is that Catherine was undoubtedly very interested in the ideas of the *philosophes* and genuinely wanted to improve her subjects' lives. She corresponded with Montesquieu, Diderot and Voltaire and even (unsuccessfully) invited the latter to Russia. When the British prison reformer John Howard appeared in Russia he was allowed access to gaols in St Petersburg, Moscow and the provinces. However, like Frederick II and Joseph II, Catherine was not doctrinaire and would not attempt changes which might endanger her throne. As this chapter will show, she was sympathetic to free trade, to ameliorating the lot of the serfs and to equality under the law, but she was careful to encourage neither peasant unrest nor noble hostility.

As early as 1767 Catherine summoned a Legislative Commission to consider a codification of the laws and she laid down in her *Nakaz*, or Instruction, what she required of it. As we shall shortly see, the *Nakaz* was heavily influenced by Enlightenment thinking, sometimes in areas which provided her with no obvious political or military advantage.

The impact of the French Revolution on Catherine

What was the French Revolution?

The French Revolution is shorthand for a complex chain of events which, beginning in the 1780s, led to the overthrow of absolute monarchy in France by late 1789, the establishment of a republic in 1792, and the seizure of power by Napoleon Bonaparte in 1799. Although the monarchy was restored in 1815, the Revolution is generally credited with establishing the concepts of **liberalism** and **nationalism** as political forces.

Although the storming of the Bastille in 1789 is commonly regarded as marking the outbreak of revolution, historians generally agree that it began with the nobles' rejection of royal taxation reforms in 1787–88. This led to a meeting of the Estates General (the French parliament) in May 1789, the first such meeting since 1614. The Estates consisted of three groups: the nobility, the clergy and the middle class, which met separately. On this occasion, the middle-class representatives invited members of the other two Estates to meet with them as a single body, to form a National Assembly with full powers to legislate for the **nation**. When Louis XVI attempted to regain control of the situation with a military coup, the Assembly was rescued by an uprising of the Paris crowd, culminating in the fall of the Bastille in July.

Louis's subsequent refusal to behave as a constitutional monarch led to radicalism among some revolutionaries, to war with Austria and Prussia in 1792, and to a republic before the end of the year. The execution of Louis in January 1793, French expansionism and France's attempts to export her revolution to all European monarchies widened the war and turned it into an ideological conflict. Spectacular French military successes between 1793 and 1796, the establishment of 'sister republics' as satellite states, and the 'Terror', a campaign of violence and intimidation against internal enemies (1793–94), all made conservative governments the more determined to oppose the French republic by all possible means.

The impact of the French Revolution upon Russian domestic affairs

No autocratic ruler, let alone one governing a multinational empire, could look upon the French Revolution with anything but foreboding. Catherine, usually very generous in her application of the censorship laws, became exceptionally draconian from 1790, when she read Alexander Radishchev's *Journey from St Petersburg to Moscow*, in which the author attacked serfdom, arbitrary government and aggressive militarism. Seeing the author's ideas as **Jacobinism**, and aware that the present system of censorship was dangerously uneven, she instituted a crackdown on radicalism. Radishchev was arrested and condemned to death, a sentence Catherine commuted to Siberian exile. Other writers were investigated and imprisoned; Voltaire's books were burnt; licences for private printing presses were revoked; and a rigorous censorship was imposed to keep poisonous French notions out of Russia. If Catherine had ever contemplated giving debate equal status with obedience, that option was now dead.

The impact upon Russian foreign affairs

In 1798 Russian forces drove the French out of Italy and invaded Switzerland, only failing in the end through lack of support from their Austrian ally. It is possible (though impossible to prove) that an earlier intervention could have checked French expansion before it really got started. However, Catherine, like her Prussian and Austrian opponents, was too concerned about the risk of war over Poland to pay much attention to France. After all, from 1789 to 1792 France appeared to be weak, bankrupt and chaotic – a situation which seemed to give the other powers unprecedented freedom of action.

ACTIVITY 4.2

Create two teams, one to argue against the use of the term 'Enlightened absolutism' and the other to argue in its favour. The rest of the class can vote to decide the outcome. This activity will require further reading about the debate. An article such as that by Malcolm Crook, listed under Further Reading, will provide a useful digest. Try looking up 'Enlightenment', 'Enlightened despot' or 'Enlightened absolutism' in the indexes of books about Catherine.

Key term

Jacobinism: the Jacobins were the French radicals who seized power in June 1793 and under whom the 'Terror' to intimidate their opponents and maximise the nation's war effort was launched. The term 'Jacobinism' was used more loosely to describe individuals and movements which adopted (or were accused of adopting) violent methods to pursue radical political change.

Developments in central and local government

Codification of the law

Legal codification was desirable for a number of reasons. The idea that whole empires should have one uniform legal system was underpinned by the notion of equality before the law. The removal of conflicting laws promised less confusion, quicker justice and, from Catherine's point of view, a big step towards her goal of administrative and cultural uniformity. To that end, she rejected Diderot's insistence on allowing a judge room to interpret the law with discretion, in favour of Voltaire's insistence that he must only apply it.

ACTIVITY 4.3

Research and construct a timeline of the key stages in the French Revolution.

Key term

Knout: a whip with multiple lashes, used for punishments (especially of serfs)

Figure 4.1: Flogging with the knout was customary, common, often prolonged and frequently fatal. Even a sympathetic ruler like Catherine could do little to ameliorate the practice.

Catherine again parted company with Diderot on the question of torture, which he advocated as a deterrent and which she, following Beccaria, condemned. She particularly disliked the use of the **knout**, a widespread form of whipping which inflicted excruciating pain and was frequently fatal. She also, at least before 1773, opposed the use of indiscriminate executions, even against rebels.

However, progress was slow, partly because the law still depended upon the will of the autocrat and was not seen as an independent and impartial source of authority.

The Great Commission

In December 1766 Catherine issued a manifesto announcing the creation of a Legislative Commission to codify the laws. There was nothing extraordinary in that: a number of such committees had been summoned in the course of the 18th century, as regime after regime grappled with the problem of legal reform. But this Commission was not to be the usual board of noble ministers and non-noble experts. It was to be an assembly representative of:

- each of the great departments of state: Senate, Colleges, Holy Synod
- each of the districts: the nobility, townsfolk and rural commoners
- each of the Cossack 'hosts' autonomous communities, e.g. the Don Cossack 'host'.

Moreover, the role of deputy was not to be yet another onerous form of service but a privilege to be sought after: deputies were to be paid salaries and granted immunity from capital or corporal punishment, including torture, for life.

It was emphatically not a parliament or a constituent assembly. Deputies were specifically forbidden to voice public grievances or lobby on behalf of their districts. When a deputy resigned, he could simply choose another to take his place – there was no requirement for a by-election – and sometimes deputies were not replaced at all. That hardly mattered as the Commission could not take decisions by voting. The word 'Legislative' in its title is therefore misleading, as

Voices from the past

John Howard, c.1726–1790

John Howard was born around 1726 in Hackney or Enfield in north-east London, to a well-off upholsterer and carpet seller with a business in Smithfield and a small estate at Cardington, near Bedford. After an education which taught him a little about spelling, grammar and foreign languages, he was apprenticed to a wholesale grocer in London. When his father died in 1742, he inherited the estate and enough money to buy himself out of his apprenticeship and go on a Grand Tour of France and Italy. In ill health for most of his life, he was a persistent traveller, in 1755 visiting Lisbon, which had been devastated by an earthquake earlier that year. While travelling, his ship was taken by a French privateer and he spent some time in prisons at Brest.

Having been released following an exchange of prisoners, he returned to England and set about improving the conditions of his tenants. His experiences also alerted him to conditions in prisons and he devoted a good deal of time to visiting and studying them, writing reports and putting forward recommendations. Statues have been put up in London, Bedford and Kherson in Ukraine, where he died.

its sole function was to provide the Empress with advice. Each deputy was given written 'instructions' by those who had elected them, but these *nakazy* often had little content. One stated that the district had nothing to complain of and wanted no new laws.

The *Nakaz*

As early as 1765 Catherine had begun to prepare the document which only later became the *Nakaz* (Instruction) for the Commission. Whether she linked the two projects in her mind from the beginning, or whether she brought them together at a later date, is unknown. She drew most of her ideas from Enlightenment writers. Of the 526 articles in the first part of the *Nakaz*, 294 came from Montesquieu's *L'Esprit des lois* (*The Spirit of the Laws*) and 108 from Cesare Beccaria's work. Early drafts of the *Nakaz* show that Catherine would have liked to have abolished serfdom, but later ones reveal that she recognised the impossibility of doing so if she wished to retain her throne.

Reform of the Senate

Catherine's collaborator, Nikita Panin, had failed to establish her as a regent for her son Paul and therefore sought other ways of limiting her power. He was also anxious to limit the influence of the Orlovs, and of Alexis Bestuzhev-Ryumin, who was working for Catherine's marriage to her current lover, Gregory Orlov. Some time in 1762 he put forward to Catherine a plan for a supreme policy-making body, an imperial council, and for a Senate reorganised and confined to administration. Catherine saw the need for reform but was not about to let her authority be restrained by a council. By early 1763 she concluded that Panin's was a minority view, dropped the idea of a council and turned instead to reform of the Senate.

In Catherine's view, the Senate had too often strayed from its proper administrative role into the realms of legislation and policy, thereby trespassing upon the sovereign's prerogative. She was also irritated by the internal squabbles between those who saw it as an instrument of centralised bureaucracy and those who thought that it should be dominated by aristocratic interests.

Voices from the past

Montesquieu, 1689–1755

Charles-Louis de Secondat, Baron of La Brède and Montesquieu, was born near Bordeaux in south-western France and educated at a Catholic school for the sons of nobles, before becoming a lawyer. However, he soon gave up legal practice for writing and published a number of influential works. His masterpiece, *L'Esprit des lois* (*The Spirit of the Laws*), was read from Moscow to North America, calling attention to the effects of environmental factors upon forms of government. Thus a moderate monarchy, in which the crown was balanced by the aristocracy and commons, was best suited to the French nation. He did not recognise the clergy as a distinct estate and held that religions, like laws, should be judged on their usefulness to society. Laws should aim to prevent harm, not to limit liberty or to inflict cruel punishments – torture, serfdom and the mistreatment of prisoners of war were thus contrary to good government. Though hereditary monarchy based on primogeniture was a key principle, he conceded that a woman could be an effective head of state, although not an effective head of a family.

ACTIVITY 4.4

Draw up a table listing the 'Enlightened' aspects of Catherine's local government reforms, against those which seem to suggest that she wished merely to maintain an effective grip on power. Which, if either, seems to predominate?

Her reform of 1763 followed Panin's plan by dividing the Senate into six departments, of which only the first two – covering the vast bulk of internal administration and judicial matters respectively – had any real significance. Each department could only consider matters allowed by existing law, and had to reach unanimous decisions. If that decision was not forthcoming, the question had to be referred to a full session of the Senate where, again, a unanimous decision was required. If unanimity proved elusive, the matter could be referred to the Empress. The effect was to relieve the monarch of routine decisions on minor matters while reserving to her the questions that mattered. To ensure that Catherine was really in control, the Procurator-General was made head of the first department and supervised the procurators of the other five. A few months later, in October, Catherine neatly sidelined senior figures in the two factions seeking to influence her. To achieve this, Bestuzhev was removed from the College of Foreign Affairs and replaced by Panin, thus depriving the latter of the vast patronage available to a minister in charge of domestic matters.

Catherine thus moved towards a system capable of executing routine business without the monarch's direct intervention, while ensuring that she alone would have real political power.

Changes to local government in towns and rural areas

As early as 1763 Catherine set about establishing a more personal grip on local administration while attempting to deal with inflexibility and peculation. In December of that year she introduced greater uniformity by defining the precise duties of each grade of official and she attacked corruption by increasing salaries. In April 1764 she gave governors greater freedom to act independently and encouraged them to correspond directly with her rather than through the Senate. Her principal aim was clearly to obtain greater personal control over local government and to downgrade the power of the Senate further.

The changes did not produce instant efficiency and the salaries were not high enough to root out long-established corruption. It was not until 1775, after the failure of the Legislative Commission and in the wake of the Pugachev revolt, that a more comprehensive reform was attempted. The resulting statute, usually known as the Provincial Reform, reorganised on population lines the boundaries of the provinces (300 000–400 000 inhabitants) and districts (20 000–30 000). In the outlying regions, where local government had so spectacularly collapsed during Pugachev's insurgency, new provinces were created, bringing the total number to 44 immediately and to 50 by 1796. In towns and in the countryside, courts were established in which nobles, peasants and townsfolk could be judged by their peers.

It was a noble effort but it fell short in terms of resources. As ever, the main and insuperable obstacle was the inadequate supply of talented officials. The total number of posts rose from 16 500 in 1762 to over 38 000 by the end of the reign. Many positions remained vacant and many others fell into the hands of minors.

Changes to society

The importance of landownership and the gentry

In 1785 Catherine issued her Charter of the Nobility, intended to clarify the relationship between nobility and autocrat.

In terms of local government it:

- recognised hitherto informal provincial assemblies of nobles;
- gave those assemblies the right to 'register' those whom they considered to be of noble rank.

It confirmed the rights of the nobility to:

- travel abroad;
- enter foreign service;
- buy serf villages (in this case an exclusive right).

It confirmed nobles' freedom from:

- compulsory state service;
- personal taxation;
- corporal punishment;
- billeting of troops in their houses.

At first sight the Charter appears revolutionary. Some historians have contended that it instituted civil rights in Russia, rights which might in time have been filtered downwards. Others have argued that it gave privileges to a tiny minority and, by confirming hereditary rights, placed Russian nobles on the same footing as their Western counterparts. Their estates, and the serfs living on them, were now their own heritable possessions forever. By finally severing the connection between service and noble status, the autocracy lost all control over the Russian aristocracy.

Those views are, however, contested by S.M. Troitsky, Isabel de Madariaga and Simon Dixon. Dixon, following the historian Robert Jones, contends that it was not revolutionary at all. It was not an agreement between two contracting parties but a unilateral declaration by the autocracy which could be revoked at will. It did not restrict the promotion of commoners to noble status through the Table of Ranks and did not cede tax-raising powers to provincial assemblies. As to the nobles' property rights over both land and serfs, Madariaga observes that 'if the Charter introduced changes in these fields, it was by omission rather than commission'.[2] The serfs are nowhere explicitly mentioned, and implicitly only in article 26, which states: 'the right of nobles to buy villages is confirmed'. Nor did the Charter change the nobles' existing rights over their serfs.

Enlightenment and education

An Enlightened absolute monarch needs to be understood for their reforms to be effective. It was one thing to introduce reforms, quite another to persuade illiterate and tradition-bound subjects to accept them. Moreover, a school which taught morality as well as knowledge would encourage obedience to constituted

ACTIVITY 4.5

'From 1785 the Russian autocracy was the prisoner of the aristocracy.' How accurate is this assessment?

authority. That, argues Dixon, is why the monarchs took the lead over the *philosophes*. Whereas Voltaire predicted that revolt and disorder would arise from universal education, Catherine considered schemes for schooling her people, for males and females, nobles and peasants. However, it took time to work out a sensible national scheme and the results were uneven.

Work began in 1764 but by 1771 neither a special education commission nor a committee of the Legislative Commission had produced a practical system. The Provincial Reform of 1775 obliged local welfare boards to establish schools, but the results depended upon the attitudes of provincial governors and local nobility. This system naturally produced very indifferent results: in 1780 Catherine, on a tour of the north-west, discovered that Pskov had a good school for nobles but nothing for townspeople. On that occasion she put her hand into her own purse to remedy the situation and in 1782 she set up a National Commission on Education. The commission's work led her to adopt a moderately conservative system already established in Prussia and the Habsburg Monarchy, and well calculated to contribute to the Empress's goal of a culturally uniform empire.

On 5 August 1786 Catherine issued a decree creating a network of free, coeducational primary and secondary schools in the towns, and primary schools in rural districts. In principle they were open to all classes, although serf children could attend only with the consent of their owners. By 1788 such schools had been opened in 26 provinces. However, most of these institutions were in or near Moscow and St Petersburg, so that provision elsewhere was lamentably thin. Five provinces had only one school each. Moreover, all provinces covered huge areas – around 10 000 square miles in the case of Smolensk. Equipment was scarce everywhere and many schools had very brief lives.

Yet there were successes. As early as May 1764 a generously endowed Foundling Hospital for sheltering and schooling abandoned children was established in Moscow. A month later, the Smolny Institute for Noble Girls opened its doors in St Petersburg. Nor was female education – a startling enough initiative in itself – confined to the aristocracy. Hard on the Smolny's heels came the Novodovechny Institute for Girls of the Third Estate. By 1800 there were over 3000 free non-compulsory schools in Russia, educating 20 000 pupils, including 2000 girls.

Reforms to religion

Catherine was, of course, officially a convert to Orthodoxy. There were plenty of signs, however, that she did not take her Orthodoxy altogether seriously. Madariaga calls her an agnostic, but Simon Dixon feels that it 'might be more revealing to think of her as a secularised Protestant'.[3] By that he seems to mean that, while her religious faith did not run very deep, her Protestant background had formed many of her attitudes. She disliked elaborate ritual and the seasonal vagaries of the Orthodox liturgy. She had a strong work ethic and placed high value upon duty and obedience – virtues she fervently wished to instil in her subjects. She had a deep dislike of monasticism: she was quite capable of doing her duty as a pilgrim at a monastic shrine in the morning and demonstrating her indifference by going hunting in the afternoon. Monks and nuns, she assumed, served no important purpose and were simply out to make money from tourists.

Where Catherine did make a striking difference was in the field of toleration, where she went even further than Joseph II and for similar reasons. Jews, Muslims, Catholics and all kinds of Protestants were welcome to live and worship freely in her empire, provided that they were loyal subjects. Loyal subjects were at a premium because it was widely believed that Russia was under-populated; and denominational differences were to be discouraged in the interests of harmony and loyalty to a beneficent autocrat.

The economy and the persistence of serfdom

The roots of economic success

Economic historians now generally agree that in Catherine's time the Russian economy became strikingly dynamic and prosperous. This seems to have been driven by a combination of an expansion of agriculture and the availability of cheap international credit.

Catherine raised the equivalent of 44 million roubles on the Amsterdam money market to finance her two wars against the Turks. Yet the debt did not become excessive, standing at 33 million in 1796, partly because the Turks were forced to repay some of it by way of indemnity. A healthy export trade in naval stores to sustain foreign navies and merchant vessels created another inflow of wealth. The influx of capital, combined with a growing population, created a powerful internal demand for food and industrial products. Rising population and access to the newly conquered and fertile lands in the south further benefited agriculture. While transportation costs across the Russian vastness were high, labour was cheap enough to compensate.

Catherine and her advisers were, however, unsure about how best to promote prosperity. Her Enlightenment reading drew her to internal free trade: she disliked monopolies and up to 1781 worked to eradicate them, with mixed success. In 1775 she broke the traditional urban stranglehold upon small-scale industry, leading landlords to encourage their serfs to engage in handicraft production for the wider market. Nobles on infertile estates north and west of Moscow were especially responsive. All this should logically have led to internal free trade, at least in grain, and to the emancipation of the serfs.

Catherine herself disliked serfdom and there are signs that she favoured abolition. In the mid-1760s she was influenced by abolitionist advisers, and in April 1766 the Free Economic Society awarded its prize for an essay on the serf problem to an abolitionist composition. There are plentiful signs of that thinking in the drafts of the *Nakaz*.

Why were the serfs not freed?

However, there were powerful considerations pulling in the opposite direction. One was Catherine's fundamental belief in the primacy of agriculture; another was the basic importance of servile labour to an overwhelming agrarian economy. The social, ideological and security motives, firmly stressed by Nikita Panin, were even more influential:

- it would be imprudent to anger the nobles by freeing their serfs;

ACTIVITY 4.6

Prepare and deliver a class presentation in answer to the following statement: 'Catherine II was never in a position to interfere with Russian serfdom'. How valid is this view? Remember to contextualise the question (Catherine, serfdom, Russia) and then to assess both sides – that she was, as well as that she was not – before declaring whether you agree or disagree with the proposition.

- a peasantry presumed to be lazy and ignorant needed close supervision;
- emancipation could bring with it uncontrollable peasant unrest;
- excessive social mobility would undermine a God-given social hierarchy;
- Russia's spectacular international success in Catherine's reign rested on an army largely composed of conscripted serfs.

Thus Catherine, always cautious, was reduced to ameliorating the lives of peasants whom she dared not liberate. On the face of it this is ammunition for those who argue that her reformist views were a mere blind for repressive autocracy. However, it is probably more accurate to see her as wavering between a basic abhorrence of serfdom and the practical problems of government and survival. She was genuinely concerned by instances of mistreatment and directly interfered in a number of such cases. However, her confirmation of the traditional rights of the nobles gave her little room for widespread reform.

Opposition and rebellion

Plots against Catherine and her reaction

Catherine was a usurper. She had no legal right to the throne and was therefore exposed to the schemes of those planning to use a plausible claimant to seize power. The three obvious claimants were:

- her late husband, Peter III (deposed, possibly assassinated in 1762 but falsely rumoured to be still living);
- her son Paul (later Paul I);
- Ivan VI (deposed by Elizabeth in 1741 and held in prison until 1764).

Plots centred on the restoration of Peter III or Ivan VI, or on the enthronement of Paul, emerged at a very early stage of Catherine's reign. In 1764 a group of Guards officers attempting to liberate Ivan were foiled only when the gaoler, obeying standing orders, strangled his prisoner. Several plots in favour of Paul were detected and snuffed out in the course of 1769–70, Catherine commuting frequently savage sentences, to exile to the Kamchatka peninsula in Siberia. In 1771 a band of these exiles killed the incompetent commandant and escaped in a commandeered ship, eventually reaching France. All these conspiracies were at the centre of power and aimed at a palace coup.

In addition to plots, there were pretenders. By John T. Alexander's reckoning, at least 24 pretenders claiming to be Peter III appeared during Catherine's reign, 10 of them during her first decade.[4] Blanning detects 'at least a dozen between 1762 and 1774, variously claiming to be Peter III, Ivan VI, a son of George III of England, the Tsarina Elizabeth, a daughter of Elizabeth and so on'.[5] There were frequent conspiracies aimed at enthroning Paul, and at least one to restore Ivan. Catherine was lucky to survive.

Whereas the plots in favour of Paul came from the elite, the pretenders usually appeared in the volatile frontier lands and were persons of humble origin. For example, in March 1772 Fedor Kazin (alias Bogonomov), a runaway serf and army deserter, convinced some Don Cossacks that he was Peter III. Arrested and imprisoned at Tsarytsin on the Volga, he was freed by a mob, rearrested,

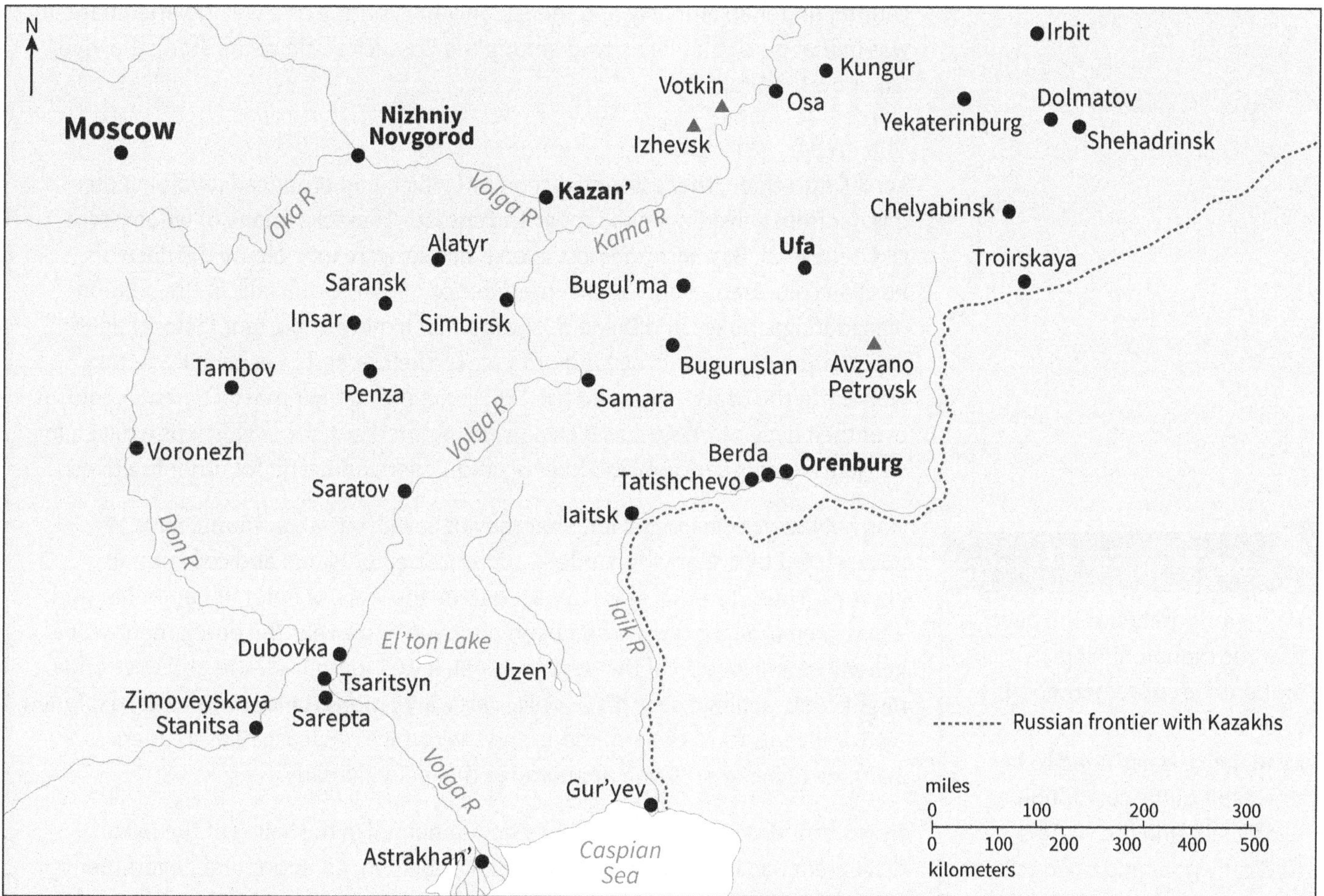

Figure 4.2: The Pugachev Revolt

whipped, branded and mutilated before dying on his way to a Siberian exile. Some of his followers turned to another pretender, the brigand leader Riazin. Others gathered around the most able, charismatic and dangerous pretender of them all: Emilian Pugachev.

The Pugachev Revolt and its consequences

Who was Pugachev?

Pugachev was a Don Cossack, born about 1742. In other words, he came not merely from a region but from a specific community with a tradition of turbulent resistance to Tsarist rule. Called up for military service at 17, he quickly attracted attention for his unusual intelligence and energy. During the Seven Years War he was commended for efficiency, and during Catherine's first war against the Turks he was commissioned as a junior lieutenant of cavalry.

However, for Pugachev, as for many others, service had its dark side. He was once severely whipped for allowing a horse to stray. On his return from the Seven Years War he was plucked again from his wife and sons for service in White Russia (now part of Belorus), before being sent to fight the Turks in 1769. Home on sick leave in 1771, he decided not to return and became a hunted deserter. Isabel de Madariaga traces his wanderings to Taganrog, the Terek River Cossacks, back to the Don country under an amnesty and thence onwards, posing as a wealthy merchant. It was in that guise that he arrived among the Cossack settlements along the River Iaik, now the Ural.

The causes of revolt

Across the region, the festering discontent which had produced revolt in Peter I's day, far from subsiding, had grown and spread. Cossacks (many of whom were Old Believers), Bashkirs and now even Kalmyks were irritated by the pace of Russian colonisation and by the interference of Tsarist officials. In the opinion of Madariaga, Dukes and Dixon this was a much more important factor than the exploitation of peasants by landlords. Nevertheless, serfs – especially factory workers in the Urals – resented the 1762 edict giving their masters greater control over their lives. Moreover, as B.H. Sumner pointed out, the region was a haven for peasants fleeing serfdom and high taxation, for bandits and for other fugitives.

Key term

Naive monarchism: the belief that the monarch (king or emperor) is supremely good and placed in authority by God. All injustice is assumed to be the result of the corruption of officials, and the victims (typically poor and uneducated) are convinced that, if only they could get a message through to the monarch, all wrongs would be righted.

Many of the people longed for what they believed was a traditional form of government by a Tsar who, under God, protected personal and communal liberties. The 1762 edict was supposed to be the work of Peter III's enemies, and it was even thought that he had been removed to prevent the proclamation of a general emancipation of the serfs. Peter III, it was rumoured, was still alive and might come again to save his people. This **naive monarchism** was easily exploited by the adventurous, the ambitious and the ruthless: at least 20 pretenders claiming to be Peter III had appeared in the region already.

By November 1772, when Pugachev first appeared in the valley of the Iaik, discontent had already flared into violent rebellion. An unpopular government inspector, General Taubenberg, and some Cossack leaders who had collaborated with the state were murdered, and the rebels needed a leader – preferably a Peter III whose presence would give the uprising legitimacy. The stranger Pugachev easily passed himself off as the returned Tsar: he was twice arrested upon suspicion of sedition before assuming command of the insurgency in 1773.

Pugachev's military aims are still unclear. His manifestos claimed that his mission was to march on Moscow and reclaim the throne, but this may have been no more than necessary propaganda. Madariaga may well be right in claiming that he meant to lead his forces into the sanctuary of the Ottoman Empire, and only when that became impossible did he turn towards the Russian interior.

The course of the Revolt

The revolt began with a proclamation aimed at bringing as wide a range of dissidents as possible into the revolt. Recruits flocked in and, although the fort at Iaitsk held out, a formidable army besieged Orenburg, the principal government stronghold on the Iaik. Far from being a formless peasant explosion, the revolt developed a rudimentary administrative system and even its own War College. It was far and away the most dangerous of all the great uprisings. Nevertheless, its fundamental weaknesses were indiscipline, lack of a clear command structure, lack of scientific siege-craft and a tactical inability to face regular troops in battle.

In 1774 fighting spread to the Urals, where Pugachev linked up with rebellious factory serfs and Bashkirs. Two of the three Tsarist forces sent against them were beaten in battle, but one of them reached Orenburg. Defeated in battle in

March, Pugachev took his main army of about 20 000 west to the Volga, where he captured Samara. Turning north, he stormed the city of Kazan in July. But before he could take the town's *kremlin* (citadel fortress), a relief force arrived. In the ensuing battles, more than one-third of Pugachev's men were killed or taken. Survivors, including nearly all the Bashkirs, abandoned him, leaving him with no more than 500 followers to lead south down the Volga.

Pugachev was heading for the Don, where he hoped to raise a new army and march on Moscow. As he went he issued an edict appealing to the Volga serfs, terrorised their landlords and rebuilt his forces. Recruits poured in from as far away as Ukraine. Panic swept through the Moscow region and through Moscow itself. Central Russia and Russian society, even the autocracy, appeared to be on the brink of collapse. Catherine had to send her best military commanders to stop the rot.

The collapse came suddenly and unexpectedly. The Don Cossacks failed to rise, and towards the end of 1774 a government army scored a crushing victory over Pugachev at Tsaritsyn on the Volga, leaving some 9000 rebels dead. Under General Panin's subsequent counter-offensive the rebel army disintegrated, and a fleeing Pugachev was betrayed by some of his own followers. Captured and hauled in an iron cage to Moscow, he was paraded through the streets on a cart before being beheaded and dismembered on 10 January 1775.

Why did Pugachev fail?

Dukes is content to put the uprising's failure down to treachery – the abrupt removal of the charismatic leader. However, Sumner detected the same weaknesses as in earlier revolts:

- Pugachev was almost illiterate;
- despite his War College, his forces were poorly coordinated and undisciplined;
- early victories against second-rate garrisons gave way to defeats at the hands of hardened regulars;
- arms, gunpowder, food and horses were in short supply;
- rebel armies were almost impossible to keep together for long;
- troops were reluctant to fight far from home;
- loyalties (as Pugachev's own fate shows) were often conditional.

The consequences of the Revolt

In the very short term, the Pugachev Revolt frightened the government and thus led to savage reprisals. Catherine became much less receptive to proposals to ameliorate serfdom and abolish retributive executions. However, there was a more constructive response, in the shape of reforms designed to strengthen local government in the regions where it had so catastrophically collapsed.

The Revolt also gave rise to a legend of heroic resistance which lived on well into the 19th century.

ACTIVITY 4.7

Make notes on the following question and use those notes as the basis of a class presentation: 'Why did the Pugachev Revolt fail?' You might want to start by drawing attention to its strengths and successes, then focus on the fact of its failure, analyse the weaknesses and assess to which of them you should attribute the Revolt's failure.

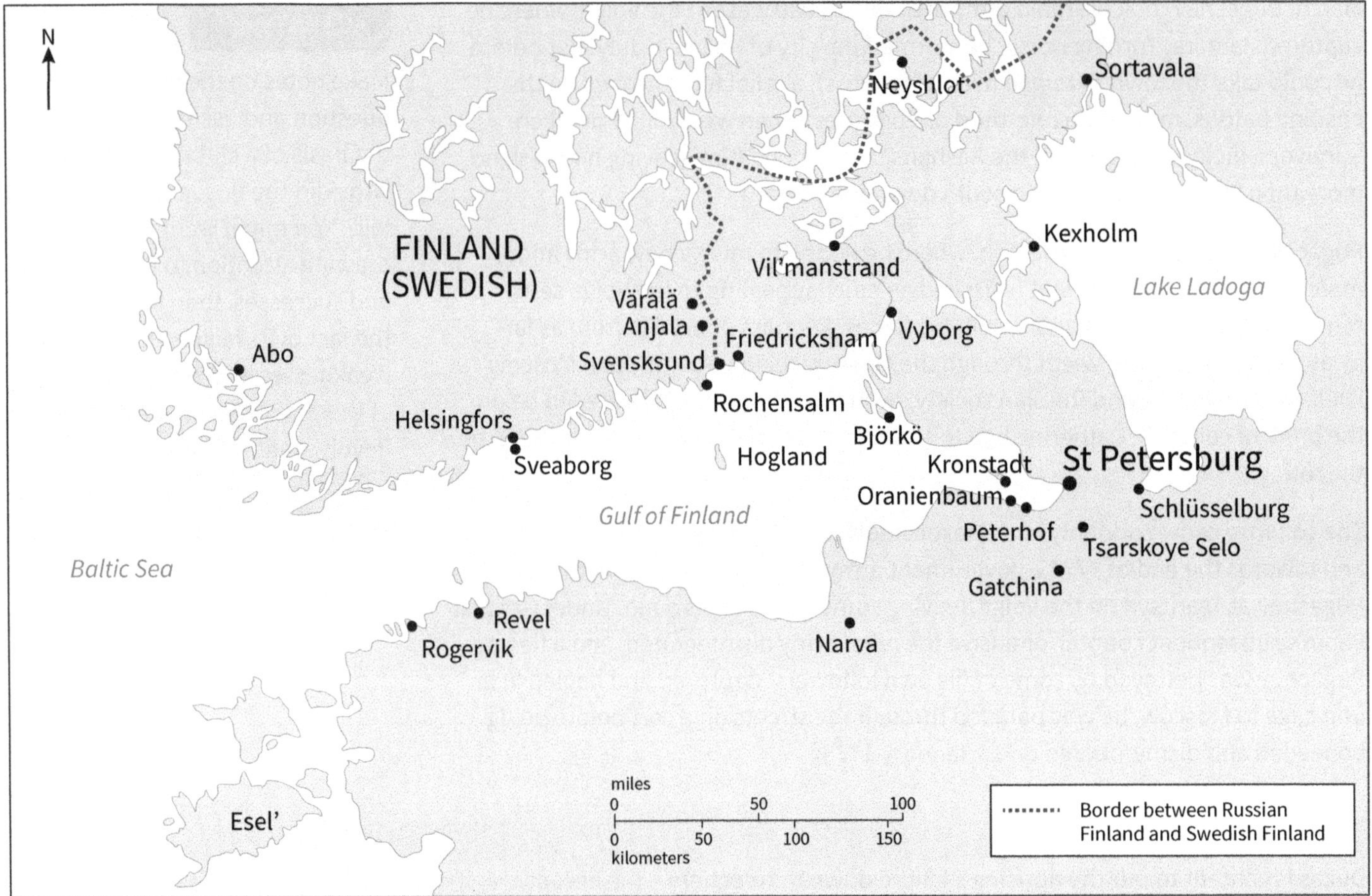

Figure 4.3: The Russo-Swedish War, 1788–1792

Foreign affairs and wars

Sweden

Sweden continued to harbour **revanchist** ambitions in the Baltic, ambitions which seemed all the more dangerous when Gustav III overthrew the constitution to establish himself as an absolute monarch. His timing was alarming because Russia was already deeply engaged in a Turkish war in the far south. However, it was not until 1788, a year after the outbreak of a second Turkish war, that Gustav resorted to arms. He seems to have been driven by his own declining popularity and by foreign powers alarmed at Russia's progress in the south.

The Swedes invaded Finland and at the same time launched a naval assault on St Petersburg. An indecisive naval battle off Hogland checked the attempt on St Petersburg, and the Swedish invasion of Finland had to be called off. Russian intrigues sparked a mutiny in the Swedish army and Catherine persuaded Denmark to invade Sweden. The Danes soon withdrew under British and Prussian threats but Catherine, with no good news from the south, spent a very anxious summer.

However, in 1789 Russian naval strength began to tell and the Swedes were forced onto the defensive. Gustav, concluding that he had very little chance of securing a victory, agreed to a peace formally concluded at Värälä on 14 August 1792.

> **Key term**
>
> **Revanchist:** from the French word for 'revenge', a revanchist is one who seeks to avenge a perceived wrong. A 'revanchist' movement sometimes develops after a military defeat, campaigning to win back lost territories.

This short and relatively insignificant conflict proved, if proof were needed, that Sweden on her own was no longer a serious threat. Nevertheless, it came at a very awkward time for Catherine and served as a reminder that over-preoccupation with the south or with Poland could leave her vulnerable in the Baltic.

Turkey and Crimea

Figure 4.4: The Russo-Turkish Wars, 1768–1774 and 1787–1792

Catherine's aims in the south were essentially those of her predecessors:

- The conquest of new territory
- The settlement of southern Ukraine
- Access to the Black Sea, through the conquest of Azov, Taganrog and Kerch
- Stable borders with the Ottomans, the Crimean Tartars, the Caucasian states and Poland.

The Russo-Turkish War, 1768–1774: causes

In 1768, Polish nobles formed the Confederation of Bar (named after the fortress where they met in conference) to defend the country against Russia, as well as against King Stanisław II Augustus, who had been placed on the throne by Catherine the Great. The prompt suppression of the Confederation and the threat of Russian intervention in Poland, both in 1768, were themselves causes of the war that then broke out between Russia and the Ottoman Empire.

The immediate trigger was a Cossack raid on the town of Balta, which belonged to the Khan of the Crimea. Encouraged by French money, the Porte declared war upon Russia on 6 October 1768.

In St Petersburg there was, not for the first time, excessive confidence born of Russian military reforms and reports of Ottoman military decline. On strategy, counsels were divided. The Panin faction wanted an immediate invasion of the

Crimea and the Ottoman Empire, while the Orlovs wanted to define Russia's strategic aims more carefully first. Gregory Orlov suggested a naval expedition from the Baltic to the Mediterranean to assault the Ottomans by sea. From these discussions a plan emerged. Two Russian armies would strike in the south, one against the Crimea and the other against the Danubian principalities.

The Russo-Turkish War, 1768–1774: events

Operations began in the spring of 1769. At first the Russians won a row of victories and Moldavia was overrun. A combination of bubonic plague in Moldavia and floods in southern Poland forced the Russians to retire, but in July they were back to inflict two crushing defeats on the Turks, conquer Moldavia and invade neighbouring Wallachia. In 1770 the Baltic fleet appeared off the Turkish coast and destroyed the Ottoman navy at Chesme. The following year Vasily Dorgoruky conquered the Crimea.

All this delighted Catherine but frightened Austria and Prussia: both occupied frontier districts of Poland. Frederick II even sent his brother Henry to St Petersburg to suggest that Poland should be divided, a proposal which Catherine accepted in 1771. Meanwhile, the Turks fought doggedly on, presenting Catherine with the prospect of war with all three powers at the same time. Consequently, in 1771 she agreed to partition Poland while opening peace talks with the Turks. Although a wider war was avoided, the peace talks failed and the Turkish conflict dragged on.

A Russian expedition across the Danube failed for want of supplies, while the fleet in the Mediterranean could do no more than raid Turkish ports and encourage Arab revolts. Only the death of Sultan Mustafa III in 1773, and the succession of his more conciliatory brother, Abdul-Hamid I, gave hope of peace. A new Russian crossing of the Danube and Alexander Suvorov's subsequent victories finally induced the Turks to negotiate.

The Treaty of Kutchuk-Kainardji, July 1774

The treaty signed at the Bulgarian village of Kutchuk-Kainardji was a Russian triumph. The Turks finally accepted the independence of the Crimea (which in practice meant Russian domination), Russian access to the Black Sea through the acquisition of Kerch and the right to navigate upon it, access to the Mediterranean via the Straits. They also agreed to Russian consular representation throughout the Ottoman Empire and to pay Russia 4.5 million roubles in reparations. Most significantly for the future, Russia was allowed to lobby the Porte in the interests of one Orthodox Church in Constantinople: a concession that Russian governments would later inflate into a right to 'protect' all the Ottomans' Orthodox subjects. In return, the Turks gained only the return of Wallachia and Moldavia.

The conquest of the Crimea, 1772–1779

The first step towards Russian domination of the Crimean khanate was taken in 1772, when Catherine struck a bargain with a charming but less-than-able Tartar prince. This was Shagin-Girei, younger brother of the elected khan, Shahib-Girei, who wanted to loosen his dependence upon the Turks. By the Treaty of Karuso Bazaar, Russia recognised Crimean independence of the Porte, accepted Shahib-Girei as Khan and pledged itself to an alliance. The effect, of course, was to turn the Crimea into a Russian puppet state – but as we have seen, it took two more years of warfare to persuade the Porte to recognise the change.

Even then the Turks had their own candidate, Devlet-Girei, who became khan (for the second time) in 1776 and then had to be removed by Russian arms in the winter of 1776–77. In installing Shagin-Girei, the Russians insisted that his authority was now absolute and hereditary, both quite alien concepts to Tartar tradition. Not surprisingly, in 1777 civil war broke out, the Ottomans tried to intervene and the new khan had to be rescued twice by Russian forces, only to be overthrown once again in the autumn of 1778. The Turks, having failed to dislodge the Russian occupying forces, agreed to a new arrangement in January 1779.

Under the Convention of Aynali Kavak they accepted Shagin-Girei as legitimate khan for life, and the independence of the Crimea in all secular matters, but in religious affairs the Sultan was recognised as Caliph. The Russians agreed to remove their forces from the Kuban and the Crimea, retaining only the key bases at Kerch, Enikale and Kinburn.

Joseph II and Catherine

War with the Turks over the Crimea was still highly probable, and Catherine looked around for a reliable ally.

- Prussia: her son Paul and her own minister Nikita Panin favoured Prussia, but Prussia had no interest in fighting the Turks.
- Austria: Prussia's foe, Austria, on the other hand, had her eyes on Ottoman territory too; and the Holy Roman Emperor, Joseph II, was hungry for conquests and glory.

In May 1780 Catherine met the Austrian emperor at Mogilev. When Joseph's mother, Maria Theresa, died in November, leaving him sole ruler of the Habsburg lands (they had previously been co-regents), Catherine immediately proposed an alliance against the Ottomans. Joseph cautiously evaded a formal treaty so that the alliance was forged through a secret exchange of letters between the two sovereigns.

- Austria would support the defence of Russia with 12 000 troops or (in the case of conflict with Sweden) 400 000 roubles a year.
- If war broke out with the Turks, Austria would respond with forces as large as the Russian ones.
- All territories gained would be divided equally.
- Neither would make a separate peace.

The agreement immediately undercut Paul and Nikita Panin, both partisans of a Prussian connection.

Shagin-Girei, the puppet khan, was more of a liability than an asset. Despotic, territorially aggressive, financially weak, lacking domestic support and ignoring Russian advice, he was again overthrown by civil war in 1780–1782. Once more Russian arms came to his rescue: Potemkin invaded the Crimea, easily dispersed the rebels and restored Shagin-Girei in October 1782.

The 'Greek Project'

At this point Catherine revived a plan, first outlined over two years earlier, to remove the Ottomans from Europe. The outcome would be two Christian buffer states between the Austrian and Russian empires: 'Dacia' in the Danubian provinces and a revived 'Greek empire' based on Constantinople. Austria would be allowed to annex the western Balkans while Russia extended her boundaries to the Black Sea, absorbing the Crimea and other coastal territories. The excuse would be the Porte's rejection of an ultimatum demanding the fulfilment of previous agreements.

Joseph was sceptical, seeing it as too ambitious and perhaps realising that the buffer states would in fact be Russian satellites. Moreover, the Turks, without allies of their own, gave in to Russian demands, thus removing any pretext for war. Potemkin formally annexed the Crimea in 1783 and the naval base of Akhtiar became Sevastopol in 1784. But Catherine, aware that the end of the War of American Independence had freed the hands of Britain and France, could do no more for the moment.

She did not get her war until 1787, by which time the Turks were both re-armed with French help and worried by Russian advances, especially in Georgia at the eastern end of the Black Sea. In August they suddenly demanded the return of the Crimea, the evacuation of Georgia and the right to search Russian ships in Turkish waters. When the Russian ambassador refused, they locked him up. Within three weeks, on 11 September, the Porte declared war. Joseph, obliged by the earlier agreement to support Catherine, and unwilling to see Russia become too strong at the expense of Turkey, immediately offered his assistance.

Catherine's war aims were to defend the Crimea and to conquer Ochakov, the Turkish fortress which choked the Dnieper estuary, opposite Kinburn and below Kherson.

The Russo-Turkish War, 1787–1792

Fighting had already begun with a seaborne Turkish offensive against Kinburn. A Russian counterattack failed and the outnumbered Russian fleet was crippled by a storm. Suvorov's garrison found themselves repulsing Turkish landings hand to hand. 'The bullet is a fool,' their commander declared, 'the bayonet a brave lad'. Far from being able to make conquests at Turkish expense, Catherine and Potemkin were faced with the likely loss of Kinburn and an unstoppable invasion of the Crimea. Potemkin advised evacuation but Catherine firmly refused her consent. In the spring of 1788 Gustav III of Sweden began to attack Russian positions in Finland, forcing Catherine to cancel a plan to send her Baltic fleet to the Mediterranean.

The tide began to turn in 1788, when Potemkin's army arrived on the Dnieper. In December Ochakov fell to assault. In 1789 Russians forces advanced to the Dniester and took Bender, while the Austrians seized Belgrade and Bucharest. Catherine, threatened by Prussia and still at war with Sweden, was now prepared to talk peace, but the Turks were in no such mood. Instead the new Sultan, Selim III, declared a holy war. In 1790 Joseph II, already facing rebellion in Hungary and the Austrian Netherlands, died, and in July his successor, Leopold II, withdrew from the war. Early in 1791 Britain threatened war unless Catherine made peace and surrendered all her conquests, including Ochakov.

But the British soon backed down, while the Russians made progress on and beyond the Danube and in the Black Sea. The Turks, despairing at last of Prussian aid, agreed to negotiate.

The Peace of Jassy, January 1792

The Peace of Jassy, signed in January 1792, recognised the Russian annexation of the Crimea and gave Catherine the territory between the Bug and Dneister rivers, including Ochakov. It was much less than Catherine had dreamed of in her 'Greek Project' and Potemkin's death during the negotiations had been a further blow. Nevertheless, it was a decisive success.

Wars with Poland and its partition

Poland had been under Russian domination from the time of Peter I, but it was not an outright possession and Poles still dreamed and schemed to free their country from Moscow's tutelage. Moreover, no less than four powers – Sweden,

ACTIVITY 4.8

Compile a short biography of Gregory Potemkin. Focus on his career, his actions and his influence over Catherine.

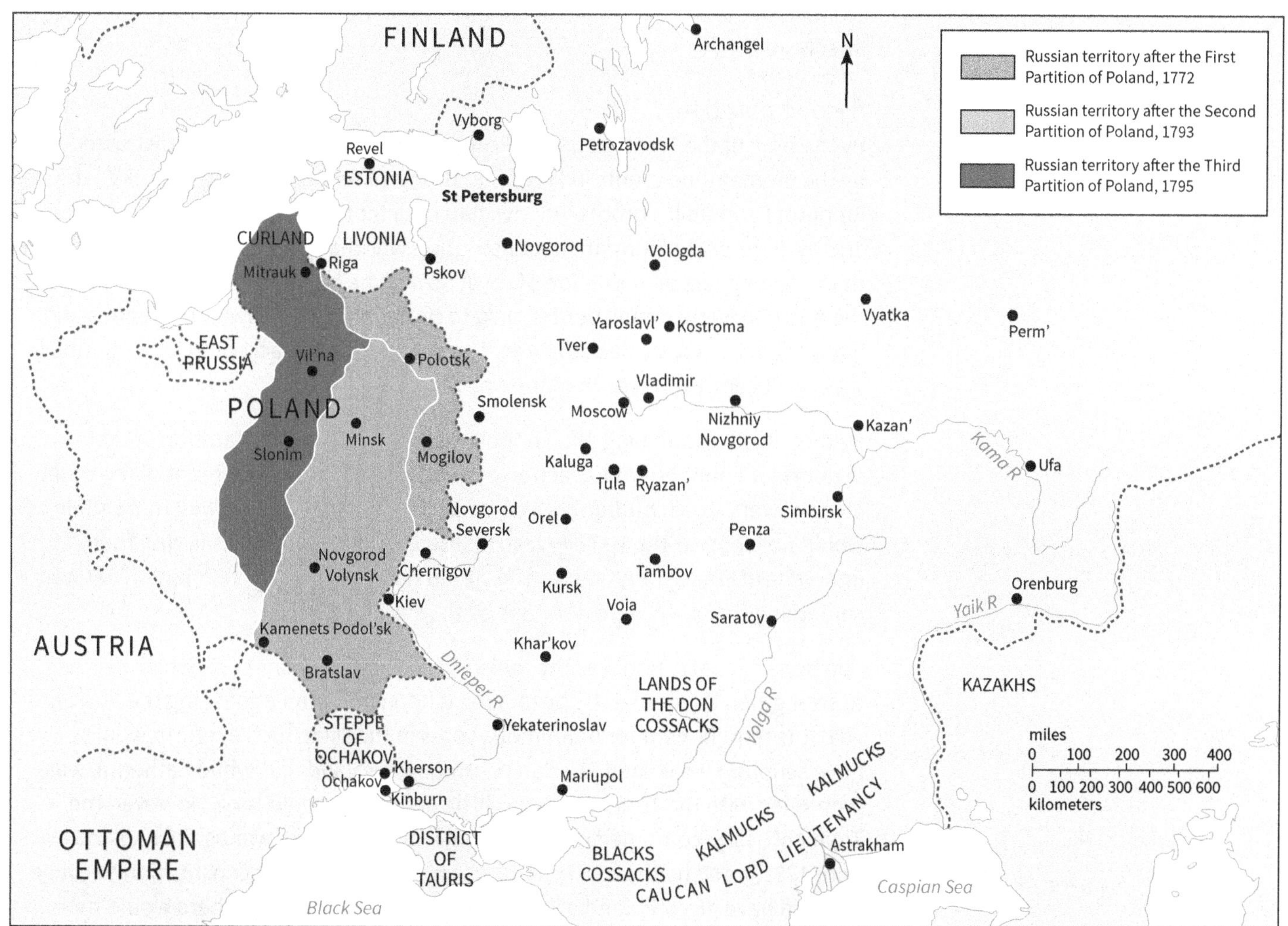

Figure 4.5: The partitions of Poland

the Ottoman Empire, the Habsburg Monarchy and Prussia – still had a keen interest in preventing a complete Russian takeover. However, at least two of them, Prussia and Austria, had no wish to see a reformed, strengthened Poland that might become a serious ally of Russia. That was exactly what Panin thought Russia should try for, but Catherine rejected his advice, probably because there could be no guarantee that a reformed Poland would remain friendly. In these circumstances an agreed partition between the three European powers was the logical solution.

First partition, 1772

As we have already seen, it was the threat of Prussian intervention while she was still at war with the Turks that persuaded Catherine to accept Frederick II of Prussia's 1771 partition proposal: Austro-Prussian mediation to end the Turkish War in return for the sliver of Polish territory separating East Prussia from Brandenburg. Austria's share was the rich province of Zips, occupied since 1769.

Russia received a wide strip of territory south of Livonia, which took its frontier up to the Dvina River in the north and embraced the whole valley of the upper Dnieper in the south. Though strategically important, this region was not apparently rich in agriculture and mineral resources, and it was once thought that Frederick had tricked the Empress. In fact, as Sumner noted, Catherine had planned this annexation a decade earlier: Frederick determined only the timing of its seizure.

Second partition, 1793

By the time of the Treaty of Jassy, Prussia and Austria had become distracted by the momentous events in France. In the summer of 1789 King Louis XVI, the Emperor Leopold II's brother-in-law, had reluctantly accepted a National Assembly and by June 1791 a permanent constitution was ready for Louis's signature. Rather than accept a radical reduction of royal powers he had fled with his family towards the Austrian Netherlands border, only to be caught at the town of Varennes and hauled ignominiously back to Paris. The constitution he accepted in September was significantly tougher than the one offered in June.

By then the Prussian king and Leopold had made a joint declaration of their support for Louis, but made action dependent upon the agreement of the other great powers. That condition was crucial. Both knew perfectly well that Britain would not support them. They also realised that Catherine was urging them to intervene in France only so that she would have a free hand in Poland. That was something that both were determined to prevent.

The bone of contention was the Polish constitution of May 1791, which set out to strengthen the monarchy by making it hereditary and abolishing the *liberum veto,* the requirement for unanimous votes in the Diet. Such a reform would have seriously weakened Russian control over Poland, but while Catherine was embroiled with the Turks there was little action she could take. However, the Treaty of Jassy, combined with the French declaration of war against Austria in April 1792, freed her hands. Prussia was hostile to the 1791 constitution because it would have given Poland a hereditary Saxon monarchy, so there would be no opposition from that quarter. Catherine immediately ordered her army into

Poland. At this point Prussia began to angle for a reward in the form of Polish territory, a move actually supported by the Austrians, who wanted to swap the Netherlands for Bavaria. The result was the partition treaty of 23 January 1793, which gave Russia the whole eastern half of Poland and 3 million people, and Prussia a much smaller but perhaps more valuable slice in the west. The Austrians got nothing: indeed, the Netherlands were overrun by France and there was no hope of winning Bavaria.

ACTIVITY 4.9

Class discussion: why was Poland partitioned?

Third partition, 1795

Patriotic Poles did not take kindly to the crushing of their constitution and the subsequent carving up of their country. In the spring of 1794 Tadeusz Kościuszco led a massive revolt, winning an unexpected initial victory over Russian forces near Cracow. But in June the Russians hit back, and in October Kościuszco was wounded and captured. The rump of Poland was about to be divided again, but this time the Austrians could not be excluded. On 24 October 1795 the three powers signed a third partition treaty – Russia's share took her right up to East Prussia and the line of the Nieman River – and Poland vanished from the map.

Timeline

1762	Catherine's seizure of power; probable death of Peter III
1764	Murder of Ivan VI
1765	Catherine begins work on the *Nakaz*
1767	First meeting of the Legislative Commission
1768–1774	War against the Turks
1772	First partition of Poland
1773–1775	Pugachev Revolt
1775	Provincial Reform
1785	Charter of the Nobility
1787–1792	War against the Turks
1793	Second partition of Poland
1795	Third partition of Poland
1796	Death of Catherine

Further reading

By now you should be able to read and enjoy sections of Simon Dixon's *Catherine the Great* (London: Pearson Education, 2001). The chapters are conveniently divided into short digestible chunks, which will help you to master both complexity and concepts. From there you may wish to go on to Isabel de Madariaga's longer and detailed, but highly readable, *Russia in the Age of Catherine the Great* (New Haven and London: Yale University Press, 1981). John T. Alexander's biography, mentioned at the end of the last chapter, scores highly on readability but may be less satisfying in terms of coverage. Malcolm Crook's article,

'Enlightened absolutism: new wine in new bottles?' in *History Review,* December 1996, 15–20, is a handy and approachable digest of the debate as it then stood.

Practice essay questions

1. How far would you agree that the Pugachev Revolt was a turning point in the reign of Catherine II?
2. 'The reign of Catherine II had no impact at all upon the standing of the Russian nobility.' How valid is this assessment?
3. How successful was Catherine in making extensive conquests at the expense of the Ottoman Empire?
4. To what extent did Catherine II participate in the partitions of Poland in order to avoid conflict with Prussia and Austria?
5. With reference to these extracts and your understanding of the historical context, which of the three extracts provides the more convincing interpretation of the summoning of the Legislative Commission in 1767?

Extract A

Why did she call a Legislative Commission of this kind? Again, we have very little evidence stemming from herself, and no records of discussions with her advisers. The most convincing explanation, on reflection, may be that Catherine and her supporters were well aware of the precariousness of her tenure of the throne. . .

Catherine may well have thought that a public and resounding endorsement of the legitimacy of her rule would strengthen her position. An assembly composed of such conflicting social groups could, with skilful management, be harnessed to her political purposes. At the same time she would be seen to be fulfilling the pledge given in the manifesto proclaiming her *coup d'état*, of devoting herself to the improvement of the machinery of government. Moreover . . . she provided at the same time an . . . opportunity for the forces of society to feel that they were participating in the political life of the country. She could also try out the subject of serfdom before a wider audience . . .

In analysing Catherine's motives, the influence of the Enlightenment must not be underestimated . . . [W]hat better way was there of demonstrating that Russia was not a 'despotism', but a genuine monarchy, than by this display of public consultation between government and society? And what better object could such a consultation have than the establishment of rational laws?

Source: Isabel de Madariaga, *Russia in the Age of Catherine the Great* (New Haven and London: Yale University Press, 1981), 161–162.

Extract B

The ostensible purpose of the commission was revealed by its title: 'Commission for the Composition of a Plan of a new Code of Laws'. It also allowed the Tsarina to gain a clearer idea of the aspirations and grievances of her non-serf subjects through the remonstrances they composed for the occasion. Catherine's most authoritative modern biographer, Isabel de Madariaga, takes the view that the information gathered as a result of the exercise proved to be 'invaluable in subsequent legislation'. That may well be so, but it is also likely that the Commission's primary purpose was to consolidate Catherine's hold on the throne: anticipating Tennyson, she knew that 'a doubtful throne is ice on summer seas'. By bringing noble deputies from all over the Empire to Moscow, she reminded the magnates of the traditional alliance between Tsars and lesser nobility. By confronting the nobility as a class with a large number of deputies from other sections of society, she attached the latter more firmly to her person and demonstrated to the former that they were not the only force in Russian society. By simply calling the Commission and having its members solemnly recognize her on her throne, she legitimized the coup of 1762 and reduced her dependence on those who had brought her to power. When the Commission had fulfilled its task, she discarded it, using the Turkish War as a convenient pretext.

Source: Tim Blanning, *The Pursuit of Glory: Europe 1648–1815* (London: Penguin, 2008) 244–245.

Extract C

In part, such contacts [with *philosophes*] were intended to propagate a favourable image of Russia in Europe, an aim in which they were largely successful. But they also reflected the empress's commitment to reason, humanity and utility.

In 1767 she placed this Enlightened trinity at the heart of her Instruction (*Nakaz*) to the Legislative Commission, a representative body convoked in a further attempt to replace the antiquated *Ulozhenie*, which the empress nevertheless admired as an edict consonant with its time and place. As Catherine openly acknowledged, her own treatise drew verbatim on Montesquieu and Beccaria. It set out her vision of a tolerant educated society in which her subjects' liberty and property would be protected by unambiguous laws established by a virtuous absolute sovereign and implemented to the letter by judges who were to assume the accused innocent until proven guilty. Never had such radical ideas been articulated in Russia. Yet, interrupted by war, the commission never completed its work. In 1775, impatient with her subjects' lukewarm response to her exhortations, Catherine resorted to direct intervention in the Petrine manner.

Source: Simon Dixon, *The Modernisation of Russia, 1676–1825* (Cambridge: Cambridge University Press, 1999), 19.

Taking it further

Why was Catherine II able to remain in power after 1762 when so many other rulers had been overthrown?

Chapter summary

After studying this chapter, you should now understand:

- Catherine's attachment to the Enlightenment and the concept of 'Enlightened absolutism'
- the extent, nature and impact of plots and rebellions against Catherine
- the extent and nature of her internal reforms
- the extent and nature of changes in the status of serfs and nobles
- the internal effects of territorial conquests
- the impact of diplomacy and war upon Russia's international standing.

You should be able to:

- evaluate the degree of internal change and continuity during the reign of Catherine II
- make informed assessments of the reasons for and extent of Russian military success and territorial expansion
- understand and weigh debates between historians of this period of Russian history.

Epilogue: Russia in 1796

When Catherine died on 5 November 1796, the Russian empire was very far from being the virtually landlocked, inward-looking, semi-barbaric state inherited by Peter the Great. The autocracy was now stronger, better armed and better financed than ever before. Yet there was still an element of insecurity: frontier wars and peasant rebellions were not infrequent and the age of palace coups was not over. In 1801 Catherine's son Paul was to die at the hands of a gang of disgruntled officers, and in 1825 Nicholas I narrowly survived a military revolt.

Russian industrial progress had been impressive: self-sufficient in weapons production, it was now the world's largest exporter of iron. However, the British industrial revolution was soon to destroy that lead. Russia was still a fundamentally conservative peasant economy, the immobile world of the Russian serf which had frustrated Peter I. Russian farming would not, on the whole, escape from three-field strip farming for over a century. Nor would modern technology, such as the horse-drawn hoes and seed-drills, long in use in Britain, take root any more easily than Peter I's scythes.

Socially too, despite the appearance of Westernisation among the landed elite, change had been sluggish. Serfdom was still a powerful institution which no Tsar dared to abolish until 1861, and then on terms which left a growing peasant population land-hungry and impoverished. And, because Russia was still an agricultural society dominated by the landlord classes, the middle class was weak. Meanwhile, the Orthodox Church was still a powerful force for continuity.

Thus, the astounding progress achieved since 1682 was balanced by a deep-rooted and stubborn conservatism. Arguably it was a dichotomy from which Russia would never escape.

End notes

1 Blanning T. *Joseph II*. London: Routledge; 1994, 83.

2 De Madariaga I. *Russia in the Age of Catherine the Great*. New Haven and London: Yale University Press; 1981, 298.

3 Dixon S. *The Modernisation of Russia*. Cambridge: Cambridge University Press; 1999, 117.

4 Alexander JT. *Catherine the Great: Life and Legend*. New York: Oxford University Press; 1989, 167.

5 Blanning T. *The Pursuit of Glory: Europe 1648–1815*. London: Penguin; 2008, 244.

Glossary

Absolutism	a system of government in which the ruler or ruling body has full powers to govern within certain limits
Agricultural revolution	a rapid change in farming methods resulting in higher productivity
Ascription (ascribe)	process whereby the government could allot serfs to a specific (government-chosen) task, even while, on paper, they remained a member of their original village
Ataman	a Cossack leader
Autocracy	a system of government in which one person (the 'autocrat') has total power
Auxiliaries	irregular troops employed alongside or instead of regular soldiers
Bandit, banditry	a bandit is an armed robber; banditry is the practice of armed robbery
Barshchina	labour services, measured in days, owed by a servant to his lord. In certain regions and for state serfs, this was commuted into a money payment, *obrok*
Blockade	military and/or naval action to prevent access to or from a fortress or port
Bondage	a socio-economic status in which the one bonded is fixed in their position by a system of inflexible rules and conventions which limit their freedom
Bourgeoisie	French term originally meaning 'town-dwellers'. In Marxist discourse it has come to mean 'industrial urban middle class'
Boyars	the highest rank of the Russian nobility
Bullion	gold or silver, usually in the form of bars, before being made into coins or other objects
Bureaucracy	a civil service, the officials employed by a government to carry out its orders
Census	a count of the population of a town, province or (usually) country
Chancellor	a leading minister responsible to the ruler
Cipher schools	schools specialising in mathematics established under Peter I
Cold War	the confrontation, without direct warfare, between the Soviet Union and its allies and the non-communist alliance led by the United States of America, between 1945 and 1989. The division affected intellectual debate, including of history
College	a committee of officials and ministers, based on the German, Danish and Swedish systems
Conditions	the terms the Council attempted to impose upon Tsarina Anna in 1730, when she succeeded to the Russian throne
Confessional state	a country in which the government supports, and is supported by, an official religion and encourages or compels its citizens to follow that religion
Conservatism	an attitude that prefers to postpone and minimise any change, and is suspicious of innovation of every kind
Cossack	a member of one of the self-governing, semi-military communities ('hosts') formed in southern Russia and Ukraine by refugees from Tsarist authority and serfdom. By the 18th century the Cossack hosts were loosely tied to the Russian state for military service.
Cottage industry	the production of goods such as yarn or cloth in rural homes rather than in factories
Coup, *coup d'état*	a sudden armed seizure of power by a small group
Doli	districts which were subdivisions of *gubernii*. The divisions were not based on natural boundaries but on population – the *doli* were drawn up in 1715 to contain precisely 5536 tax-paying households
Dragoons	originally foot soldiers who rode to the battlefield but dismounted to fight. By the 18th century they were essentially cavalry able to fight on foot as well as on horseback
Duma	Russian council of nobles
Dvoriane	Russian landlord class, comprising the titled nobility and the untitled gentry

Elector, electress a member of the small group of German nobility with the traditional power to elect the Holy Roman Emperor. By the 18th century this title effectively belonged to the Habsburg family and the election was a formality.

Elite a dominant social, political or occupational group. The Russian nobility, the senior members of the bureaucracy and the Guards regiments could all be described as elites

Embezzle to covertly steal money entrusted to one's care, often by falsifying accounts

Enlightened absolutism a form of government in which the ruler followed the principles of the Enlightenment

Enlightenment the name given to an intellectual movement of the 18th century which emphasised the improvement of the human condition through the application of reason

Expansionist one who wishes his country to acquire more territory

Expropriate to seize the property of a private individual or institution

Ferrous iron or using or containing iron; 'non-ferrous' – excluding iron

Fiskals secret administrative policemen charged with spying

Forced industrialisation industrialisation through state planning, compulsion and conscription

Galleys light vessels equipped with fore-and-aft sails and oars, enabling them to manoeuvre in light or unfavourable winds or in calms

Grand Vizier the Ottoman Sultan's chief minister

Great Embassy Peter I's journey to the West, 1697–98

Gubernii eight administrative areas into which Russia was divided in 1708. Another three were added in 1713–14

Habsburg Monarchy the territories governed by the Archdukes of Austria, who were members of the Hapsburg family. Some of these territories, such as Austria and Bohemia, were within the Holy Roman Empire; others, such as Hungary, were not

'Hat' party a Swedish political group, named after their three-corned hats, that was active from 1719-1772 and ruled Sweden between 1738-1765. Their policy of peace with France and war with Russia, led to two expensive and disastrous wars in 1740s and 1750s.

Hetman a Ukrainian leader

Hierarchy a social or political system composed of grades or ranks arranged one above another

Holy League an Austro-Polish-Venetian alliance formed in 1684 against the Ottoman Empire

Imposts taxes, usually customs duties

Indirect taxes taxes levied upon goods and services rather than directly on property or income. Customs duties are taxes

Infantry soldiers who march and fight on foot

Internal exile a punishment in which someone is forced to live far from their own home, usually at a considerable distance from urban centres, particularly from centres of culture and political decision-making

Intriguer one engaged in intrigue or secret plotting

Jacobinism the Jacobins were the French radicals who seized power in June 1793 and under whom the 'Terror' to intimidate their opponents and maximise the nation's war effort was launched. The term 'Jacobinism' was used more loosely to describe individuals and movements which adopted (or were accused of adopting) violent methods to pursue radical political change

Janissaries elite Turkish troops, technically slaves of the Sultan recruited from Christian subjects and converted to Islam. Like Guards regiments in 18th-century Russia, they could sometimes overthrow a Sultan or determine the succession through a palace coup

Khanate a kingdom ruled by a khan, usually in southern or eastern Russia, usually Muslim, usually Mongol or Tartar foundations

Kholopy slaves

Knout a whip with multiple lashes, used for punishments (especially of serfs)

Kremlin Russian word for fortress. 'The Kremlin' is the fortress which became the centre of political power in Moscow

Lancer a cavalry soldier armed with a lance, a kind of light spear

Legislative Commission a body set up by Catherine II to discuss reform of the Russian legal system

Levy the raising of a specified tax or number of troops by government order

Liberalism the principle of government through elected representatives of the people, the 'nation', with individual civil rights such as freedom of expression, association and assembly, and the security of private property. Liberals tended to want political rights for propertied men, not for the poor and landless or for women

Limited monarchy a kingdom in which the ruler shares some power with an elected assembly

Mercantilism a policy of favouring the protection of home industries through heavy tariffs upon foreign goods and heavy subsidies for home (and colonial) production

Metallurgy the working and production of metals

Metropolitan in the Orthodox Church, a senior bishop ranking between Patriarch and archbishop

Modernisation the process by which a state emerges from a largely agricultural economy, with industrial production limited to cottage industry for local consumption, to one based on large-scale production in factories, accompanied by urbanisation and the growth of an industrial middle class of businessmen and bankers, together with an industrial working class (or 'proletariat') to work in the factories and mines

Monastyriskii Prikaz the government Monastery Department, instituted in 1701

Monopoly any business which, legally or in practice, has sole right to trade in a particular market. Under Peter I a number of fledgling Russian industries were legal monopolies

Muscovy the area around Moscow, originally a dukedom

Musket a long, smooth-bored, muzzle-loading infantry firearm

Naive monarchism the belief that the monarch (king or emperor) is supremely good and placed in authority by God. All injustice is assumed to be the result of the corruption of officials, and the victims (typically poor and uneducated) are convinced that, if only they could get a message through to the monarch, all wrongs would be righted

Nakaz Instruction

Nation conventionally a people with a common cultural, linguistic and ethnic identity. This is not the same as a 'nation-state'. Most states contain several languages, cultures and ethnicities. Many nations have not formed states but are part of one or more countries

National Commission on Education a body established by Catherine II to devise a national system of instruction for Russia

Nationalism the idea that each nation should have its own state, a 'nation-state'; the attempt to defend the interests of a nation against supposed threats, typically from 'foreigners' at home or abroad

Nine Years War war in which England, the Dutch Republic and Austria fought to check the expansionist aims of Louis XIV of France, 1689–1697

Ober-Prokuror an official appointed to watch over the Synod

Obrok a form of poll tax paid by assigned serfs while away from their owner's property and thus unable to perform the usual labour services

Odnodvortsy lowest-ranking group of single-household gentry, later reclassified as peasants

Old Believers Christians who rejected Patriarch Nikon's reforms of the Russian Orthodox Church

Oligarchy a system of government which concentrates all power in the hands of a small group of individuals. It is often perpetuated by retaining that power within a network of those few individuals' families

Order of Naval Service disciplinary and signal manual produced by Peter the Great

Orthodox Christianity the Eastern branch of Christianity which formally separated from the Roman Catholic Church in the 11th century after centuries of undeclared drifting apart

Ottoman the dynasty which governed the Turkish Empire. Often used as a name for the regime and for the empire itself

Patriarch the priest at the head of the Russian Orthodox Church

Patrimonial state one in which the government has control over both public and private property, so that the two become almost indistinguishable.

Peculation embezzlement, or stealing of money entrusted to one's care

Petrine an adjective describing things to do with a 'Peter'. In Russian history, this invariably means Peter the Great. 'Pre-Petrine' – before Peter the Great

Pikes Spear-like infantry weapons up to 18 feet long, used to repel cavalry, protect musketeers and engage enemy infantry. By the late 17th century the pike was giving way to the bayonet. Boarding pikes were much shorter weapons used for hand-to-hand fighting at sea

Polarity a situation in which two sets of ideas or groups are completely opposed to each other. It suggests that there is little or no middle ground

Poll tax a tax paid by every adult. Based on a 'head count', the term comes from an old-fashioned word for 'head'

Pood a Russian measure of weight equivalent to about 36 lbs or 16.3 kg

Porte the name of the court of the Ottoman Sultan at Constantinople. It is often used as shorthand for the Turkish government that met there, rather as 'Versailles' is used in relation the France in this period, or 'Downing Street' in today's UK.

Preobrazhensky the name given to the most prominent of the Russian Guards regiments formed under Peter I

Prikhazy ministries

Primogeniture inheritance by the eldest son or, failing that, the closest male relative, all sons taking precedence over daughters.

Proletariat industrial urban working class

Provincial Reform the law restructuring local government in Russia, introduced by Catherine II in 1775

Ratusha an office introduced by Peter the Great, for the collection of revenues from the towns

Reactionary a conservative who wishes to reverse change as opposed to merely limiting or postponing it

Regent one who exercises royal powers during the minority, absence or incapacity of a living monarch

Republicanism a political view which wishes to see the abolition or removal or monarchy and its replacement with a democratically chosen head of state, a president

Revanchist from the French word for 'revenge', a revanchist is one who seeks to avenge a perceived wrong. A 'revanchist' movement sometimes develops after a military defeat, campaigning to win back lost territories

Revisionists historians who challenge earlier interpretations, especially Marxist ones

Rouble the Russian unit of currency, sometimes rendered as 'ruble'

Secret Chancellery the political police

Secular outside the authority of the Church

Semenovsky Guards the second of the two Guards regiments founded by Peter I

Serf, serfdom a serf is an unfree peasant, bound to their lord's estate. They have limited freedom of movement but are not slaves. They are obliged to provide labour and other services to the landowner

Service nobility landowners who had to perform compulsory service to the state (in the civil service or as military officers)

Seven Years War a worldwide conflict fought between European powers between 1756 and 1763. Britain, Prussia and Russia contended against France, Austria and (from 1762) Spain

Skerry boats very small coastal sailing vessels of Swedish origin, equipped with both fore-and-aft sails and oars

Slaves labourers who are held as property. Their owner has an unmitigated right to their labour. The owner has power of life and death over their slaves. Slaves tend to have no rights under law, holding a social and legal status comparable to that of draft animals in Britain before the introduction of laws against animal cruelty

Sloboda a self-governing colonial settlement, usually established by Cossacks

Smelting heating metal ore in a furnace to separate the molten metal from the rock

Soul tax a poll tax introduced in Russia in 1724

Stadtholder the head of state in the federation known as the United Provinces or the Dutch Republic.

Steppe temperate grassland

Stolnik a privileged servant

Streltsy the outdated Russian military units, with special privileges, abolished by Peter I

Strip farming a system which allotted villagers small parcels of land in each of three large fields. This was fair in that it ensured that everyone had a share of the better and worse land. It was also inefficient, since everyone's land was scattered in pieces, thus reducing yield

Subsidies payments made by the state to support home industries

Supreme Privy Council, Supreme State Council a council, at first advisory, which took over direction of government from the Senate and the presidents of the Colleges. After Catherine's death it was expanded to eight members, six of whom were drawn from the Golytsin and Dolgoruky families, the other two positions being retained by Ostermann and Golovkin.

Synod a church council. In Russia, the government department which controlled the Church

Table of Ranks a system, introduced by Peter I, of making rank in the nobility dependent upon rank in the military or civil service

Taiga a coniferous forest

Tariff a tax placed on imported goods

Third Rome a term used for Moscow, or Muscovy. After the fall of Rome and then (in 1453) of Constantinople, and the end of the empires based on those cities, many Orthodox considered Moscow to be the last bastion of true Christianity

Three-field system a system in which two fields were planted with different crops, while a third one was left unused or 'fallow'. This cyclically allowed each field one year off in three and helped avoid exhausting the soil through over-farming

Tsar a Russian word, sometimes translated as 'emperor'

Tsarevitch a Tsar's son. Later practice limited the term to the eldest son, the heir to the throne

Tundra a treeless region where the subsoil is frozen all the year round

Uezdy districts which were subdivisions of *gubernii*. The divisions were traditionally based on natural boundaries

Ulozhenie the 17th-century Russian civil law system

Uniate Church Catholic churches that followed the Orthodox liturgy

Usurper holder of a (particularly political) position who has no legal right to it

Voevody provincial governors

Westernisation the adoption of Western European ideas, technology manners, languages and customs

Zemsky zobor 'Assembly of the Land'. An elected body containing representatives of Church, nobility, towns and even some peasantry

Bibliography

Alexander, John T. *Catherine the Great: Life and Legend*, Oxford University Press, 1989

Anderson, M.S. *Peter the Great*, 2nd edition, London, Routledge, 2000

Blanc, Simone, 'The Economic Policy of Peter the Great', in W.L. Blackwell, ed., *Russian Economic Development from Peter the Great to Stalin*, New York, 1974; 21–49

Blanning, Tim, *The Pursuit of Glory: Europe 1648–1815*, London, Penguin, 2008

Bushkovitch, Paul, 'Peter the Great and the Northern War', in Dominic Leven, ed., *The Cambridge History of Russia: Volume II: Imperial Russia 1689–1917*, Cambridge, Cambridge University Press, 2006: 492–493

Cracraft, James, ed., *Peter the Great Transforms Russia*, Houghton Mifflin, 1991

Crook, Malcolm, 'Enlightened Absolutism: New Wine in New Bottles?', *History Review*, December 1996: 15–20

Dixon, Simon, *Catherine the Great*, London, Profile Books, 2010

Dixon, Simon, *The Modernisation of Russia, 1676–1825*, Cambridge, Cambridge University Press, 1999

Dukes, Paul, *The Making of Russian Absolutism, 1613–1801*, Longman, 1982

Falkus, M.E. 'The Beginnings of Industrialization', in James Cracraft, ed., *Peter the Great Transforms Russia*, Houghton Mifflin, 1991: 115–119

Fuller, J.F.C. *A Military History of the Western World Vol 2*, Boston, Mass., Da Capo Press reprint edition, 1987

Gerschenkron, Alexander, 'Russian Mercantilism: A Specific Pattern of Economic Development', in James Cracraft, ed., *Peter the Great Transforms Russia*, Houghton Mifflin, 1991: 139–158

Hughes, Lindsey, *Russia in the Age of Peter the Great*, New Haven and London, Yale University Press, 1998

Jones, Robert, *The Emancipation of the Russian Nobility 1762–85*, Princeton University Press, 1973

Klyuchevsky, Vasily Osipovich, *Peter the Great*, Beacon Press, 1984

Lee, S.J. *Peter the Great*, Routledge, 1993

Madariaga, Isabel de, *Russia in the Age of Catherine the Great*, Yale University Press, 1981

Massie, Robert K. *Peter the Great: The Compelling Story of the Man Who Created Modern Russia, Founded St Petersburg and Made His Country Part of Europe*, Head of Zeus, 2012

Moon, David, 'Peasants and Agriculture', in Dominic Lieven, ed., *The Cambridge History of Russia: Volume II: Imperial Russia 1689–1917*, Cambridge, Cambridge University Press, 2015: 369–393

Moon, David, *The Russian Peasantry: The World the Peasants Made*, London, Routledge,1999

Pipes, Richard, *Russia under the Old Regime*, 2nd edition, Penguin, 1995

Riasanovsky, Nicolai (Nicholas), 'The Image of Peter the Great', in James Cracraft, ed., *Peter the Great Transforms Russia*, D.C. Heath, 1991: 273–276

Sumner, B.H. *Survey of Russian History*, York, Methuen, 1961

Treasure, Geoffrey, *The Making of Modern Europe, 1648–1780*, London, Routledge, 2003

Yanov, Alexander, *The Russian Challenge*, Oxford, Wiley-Blackwell, 1987

Acknowledgements

The authors and publishers acknowledge the following sources of copyright material and are grateful for the permissions granted. While every effort has been made, it has not always been possible to identify the sources of all the material used, or to trace all copyright holders. If any omissions are brought to our notice, we will be happy to include the appropriate acknowledgements on reprinting.

The publisher would like to thank the following for permission to reproduce their photographs

Cover Photo, Walter Bibikow /JAI /Corbis: **p11**, INTERFOTO / Alamy Stock Photo: **p12**, Kremlin Museums, Moscow, Russia / Hirmer Fotoarchiv / Bridgeman Images: **p28**, Portrait of Augustus II the Strong as King of Poland, 1725-30, Silvestre, Louis de (1675-1760) / Deutsches Historisches Museum, Berlin, Germany / © DHM / Bridgeman Images: **p30**, Photos 12 / Alamy Stock Photo: **p34**, Heritage Image Partnership Ltd / Alamy Stock Photo: **p38**, Print Collector / Getty Images: **p42**, SPUTNIK / Alamy Stock Photo: **p50**, Heritage Image Partnership Ltd / Alamy Stock Photo: **p57**, Heritage Image Partnership Ltd / Alamy Stock Photo: **p61**, Corbis: **p66**, Pictorial Press Ltd / Alamy Stock Photo: **p68**, INTERFOTO / Alamy Stock Photo: **p69**, Tretyakov Gallery, Moscow, Russia / Bridgeman Images: **p70**, Heritage Image Partnership Ltd / Alamy Stock Photo: **p71** Heritage Image Partnership Ltd / Alamy Stock Photo: **p89**, Heritage Image Partnership Ltd / Alamy Stock Photo: **p93**, Heritage Image Partnership Ltd / Alamy Stock Photo: **p98**,

The publisher would like to thank the following for permission to reproduce extracts from their texts:

Chapter 1 Extract A p32 Peter the Great and the Northern War by P.Bushkovitch, in D.Leven (ed.) The Cambridge History of Russia: Volume II: Imperial Russia 1689-1917 © 2006 with permission of Cambridge University Press; **Chapter 2 p58** Peter the Great: his Life and Work by R.K. Massie reproduced with permission of Head of Zeus; **Chapter 2 Extract A p63** Peter the Great: his Life and Work by R.K. Massie reproduced with permission of Head of Zeus; **Chapter 3 Extract B p.90** The Making of Modern Europe 1648-1780 by G Treasure © 1985 with permission of Routledge;

Index

Lightning Source UK Ltd.
Milton Keynes UK
UKOW07f0813211016

285811UK00009B/23/P

9 781316 504352